110639867

DATE DUE

ADLAI E. STEVENSON HIGH SCHOOL
THE LIBRARY
ONE STEVENSON DRIVE
LINCOLNSHIRE, IL 60069

Death and Dying

Other books in the Social Issues Firsthand series:

Death and Dying

Sonja Eubanks, Book Editor

GREENHAVEN PRESS

An imprint of Thomson Gale, a part of The Thomson Corporation

Detroit • New York • San Francisco • New Haven, Conn. • Waterville, Maine • London

Bonnie Szumski, *Publisher*
Helen Cothran, *Managing Editor*

© 2006 Thomson Gale, a part of The Thomson Corporation.

Thomson and Star logo are trademarks and Gale and Greenhaven Press are registered trademarks used herein under license.

For more information, contact:
Greenhaven Press
27500 Drake Rd.
Farmington Hills, MI 48331-3535
Or you can visit our Internet site at http://www.gale.com

Articles in Greenhaven Press anthologies are often edited for length to meet page require-ments. In addition, original titles of these works are changed to clearly present the main thesis and to explicitly indicate the author's opinion. Every effort is made to ensure that Greenhaven Press accurately reflects the original intent of the authors. Every effort has been made to trace the owners of copyrighted material.

Cover photograph reproduced by permission of Mark Jenkinson/CORBIS.

LIBRARY OF CONGRESS CATALOGING-IN-PUBLICATION DATA

Death and dying / Sonja Eubanks, book editor.
   p. cm. -- (Social issues firsthand)
  Includes bibliographical references and index.
  ISBN 0-7377-2885-X (hardcover lib. : alk. paper)
  1. Death--Psychological aspects. 2. Bereavement. 3. Near-death experiences. I. Eubanks, Sonja, 1971– II. Series.
  BF789.D4.D3453 2007
  155.9'37--dc22

                             2006016739

Printed in the United States of America
10 9 8 7 6 5 4 3 2 1

Contents

Chapter 3: Choosing the Moment of Death

Chapter 4: Near-Death Experiences and the Afterlife

Foreword

Social issues are often viewed in abstract terms. Pressing challenges such as poverty, homelessness, and addiction are viewed as problems to be defined and solved. Politicians, social scientists, and other experts engage in debates about the extent of the problems, their causes, and how best to remedy them. Often overlooked in these discussions is the human dimension of the issue. Behind every policy debate over poverty, homelessness, and substance abuse, for example, are real people struggling to make ends meet, to survive life on the streets, and to overcome addiction to drugs and alcohol. Their stories are ubiquitous and compelling. They are the stories of everyday people—perhaps your own family members or friends—and yet they rarely influence the debates taking place in state capitols, the national Congress, or the courts.

The disparity between the public debate and private experience of social issues is well illustrated by looking at the topic of poverty. Each year the U.S. Census Bureau establishes a poverty threshold. A household with an income below the threshold is defined as poor, while a household with an income above the threshold is considered able to live on a basic subsistence level. For example, in 2003 a family of two was considered poor if its income was less than $12,015; a family of four was defined as poor if its income was less than $18,810. Based on this system, the bureau estimates that 35.9 million Americans (12.5 percent of the population) lived below the poverty line in 2003, including 12.9 million children below the age of eighteen.

Commentators disagree about what these statistics mean. Social activists insist that the huge number of officially poor Americans translates into human suffering. Even many families that have incomes above the threshold, they maintain, are likely to be struggling to get by. Other commentators insist

9

that the statistics exaggerate the problem of poverty in the United States. Compared to people in developing countries, they point out, most so-called poor families have a high quality of life. As stated by journalist Fidelis Iyebote, "Cars are owned by 70 percent of 'poor' households. . . . Color televisions belong to 97 percent of the 'poor' [and] videocassette recorders belong to nearly 75 percent. . . . Sixty-four percent have microwave ovens, half own a stereo system, and over a quarter possess an automatic dishwasher."

However, this debate over the poverty threshold and what it means is likely irrelevant to a person living in poverty. Simply put, poor people do not need the government to tell them whether they are poor. They can see it in the stack of bills they cannot pay. They are aware of it when they are forced to choose between paying rent or buying food for their children. They become painfully conscious of it when they lose their homes and are forced to live in their cars or on the streets. Indeed, the written stories of poor people define the meaning of poverty more vividly than a government bureaucracy could ever hope to. Narratives composed by the poor describe losing jobs due to injury or mental illness, depict horrific tales of childhood abuse and spousal violence, recount the loss of friends and family members. They evoke the slipping away of social supports and government assistance, the descent into substance abuse and addiction, the harsh realities of life on the streets. These are the perspectives on poverty that are too often omitted from discussions over the extent of the problem and how to solve it.

Greenhaven Press's Social Issues Firsthand series provides a forum for the often-overlooked human perspectives on society's most divisive topics of debate. Each volume focuses on one social issue and presents a collection of ten to sixteen narratives by those who have had personal involvement with the topic. Extra care has been taken to include a diverse range of perspectives. For example, in the volume on adoption, readers will find the stories of birth parents who have made an adoption plan, adoptive parents, and adoptees themselves. After exposure to these varied points of view, the reader will have a clearer understanding that adoption is an intense, emotional experience full of joyous highs and painful lows for all concerned.

The debate surrounding embryonic stem cell research illustrates the moral and ethical pressure that the public brings to bear on the scientific community. However, while nonexperts often criticize scientists for not considering the potential negative impact of their work, ironically the public's reaction against such discoveries can produce harmful results as well. For example, although the outcry against embryonic stem cell research in the United States has resulted in fewer embryos being destroyed, those with Parkinson's, such as actor Michael J. Fox, have argued that prohibiting the development of new stem cell lines ultimately will prevent a timely cure for the disease that is killing Fox and thousands of others.

Each book in the series contains several features that enhance its usefulness, including an in-depth introduction, an annotated table of contents, bibliographies for further research, a list of organizations to contact, and a thorough index. These elements—combined with the poignant voices of people touched by tragedy and triumph—make the Social Issues Firsthand series a valuable resource for research on today's topics of political discussion.

Introduction

"Nothing lasts forever. Success and failure, pleasure and pain, joy and sorrow, even beauty and love—all have their day and are gone. Memories survive longer, but in an altered, reconstructed form, resembling but not faithfully recording their origins. Personal identity is also changed over time. Nobody lives forever, and as we grow older, our appearance, feelings and functioning are changed and eventually disappear as well. One day we die, and all that is left to remind others that we once lived in this house, walked in this street, and spoke in a voice that proclaimed our existence are a few faded pictures, a memento or two, a bit of property, and the good and bad thoughts that we left in the minds of those with whom we lived, worked, played and loved."[1]

Death comes to all in its time. It is the universal truth of our existence as living beings, yet people seem to handle the inevitability of death differently. Some have said that the way one views death is a product of the culture one lives in and is a learned reaction. Still, people in all cultures and in all times have communicated certain fears about death. The fears that grip a particular individual may vary, but some fears are common to many.

For some, the fear of death is centered on the dying process. Most people have a natural instinct for self-preservation and therefore fear the process of disease, illness, and decay. With disease and illness often comes physical pain, which may be the most common fear related to death. Individuals who are dealing with disease, illness, and pain often become isolated from others, and thus some fear the loneliness of dying. For some, the fears that are most prominent have to do with a sense of helplessness and loss of power and control as disease and illness run their course and overtake the once strong and healthy body. For others, the dying process brings up fears and regrets about personal life goals that were not met.

For some, fears are more focused around being dead. People fear the loss of the life that has become so familiar and entering into the realm of the unknown. For many, the greatest fear and sadness come from the prospect of being separated from loved ones. Others fear the decay of the body after death. Some view death as a finality in which a person is destroyed and becomes a nonbeing. Others fear what will happen to them after death. Will there be punishment for acts committed during life?

People's outlooks and beliefs can affect their fear of death. People who have lived satisfying lives or who believe death is a natural part of life tend to have less fear of death. In addition, people who believe in some type of afterlife—where they will live on in spirit, in some other type of body, or in another place—seem to have fewer and less intense fears about death. Those who believe that they will be reunited with loved ones in death also have less fear of the end.

On the other hand, those who are dissatisfied with their lives, who view death as an enemy and their own decline as a personal failure, are likelier to fear death. In addition, people who believe in an afterlife but think it is a place where punishment is doled out have stronger fears about death.

Religious faith often influences beliefs about the afterlife. In general, people with firm beliefs—whether they believe strongly in God and the afterlife or that there is no God or afterlife—fear death less than those who are uncertain about what they believe regarding these matters.

Denial is a common reaction to fears about death. One manifestation of this denial is the use of different words for death, such as "passed away, deceased or expired."[2] These euphemistic words are attempts to soften the harshness that may be associated with death. Likewise, it is common in many cultures to make the dead person appear asleep rather than dead and to have brief funerals to minimize the presence of death. In modern cultures, death is largely removed from our experience because most people die in hospitals under the care of physicians who use medications to ease the pain. Other manifestations of denial include the tendency to overestimate the length of our lives and to underestimate the chance for illness and death.

Another coping strategy for many people is to find a way to transcend death. Most people want to leave some legacy behind after death. For some, the legacy is being remembered for certain accomplishments or personality traits. Some desire to be remembered because of the special relationships with others during life, such as being a good mother, father, son, or daughter. Some find meaning in being remembered for professional activities or contributions to society, whether material or through service. Some would like to be remembered for their reputations or possessions left behind to others. Some leave their legacy in the form of writings, such as poems, an autobiography, or a diary.

Death is the great unknown that all face in this life. Different people fear different aspects of the dying process, but almost all people have strong thoughts and feelings about death. These feelings may be affected by the culture a person lives in, personal beliefs about what comes after death, personal experiences with death over the course of their lives, or many other factors. People as individuals and as societies find ways to cope with death, either through denying it as a reality, denying its eminence, or looking for ways to leave a part of themselves in this life. While death seems to loom over people from the time of birth on, it has also been said that "it is the fact of death that gives life its value."[3]

Notes

1. Lewis R. Aiken, *Dying, Death, and Bereavement*. Mahwah, NJ: Lawrence Erlbaum, 2001, p. 252.
2. Clifton D. Bryant, *Handbook of Death and Dying*. Thousand Oaks, CA: Sage, 2003, p. 35.
3. Bryant, *Handbook of Death and Dying*, p. 9.

SOCIAL ISSUES
FIRSTHAND

Dealing with the Loss
of a Loved One

Comfort in a Dying Mother's List of Reasons to Live

Shoshanna Addley

Dealing with the death of a parent is often one of life's biggest challenges. In this piece Shoshanna Addley finds a list of reasons to live that her mother wrote during the last year of her life as she struggled with a terminal illness. The list provides a connection with her mother that Addley desperately needs as she deals with her loss. It also helps her understand that even though she and her mother were very different, they were quite similar in the values they held most dear, such as love, knowledge, and beauty. Shoshanna Addley is a freelance writer in Toronto, Canada, who is currently a content producer and editor for a company called Indelible Ink.

From between the yellowed pages of *The Family of Man*, a book of black and white photography from 1955, a single sheet of paper fluttered to the floor.

Curious, I crouched down and opened it. It was a list called Reasons to Live, with 10 items written in red pen, the i's dotted some time later in blue. As I scanned it, that rainy day about a year after my mother's death, I began to realize that what appeared to be just one more of her many lists, was, in fact, so much more. It was a legacy; it was a list to live by.

And the fact that it had revealed itself in the middle of a great sea of papers and books? Well, as my mom would surely say, that's serendipity.

My loving and brilliant, crazy-making and unconventional mother was a life-long maker of lists, and wrote poetry and philosophy as if they were extreme sports. She'd scribbled on anything she could get her hands on. Observations in the margins of books of fiction, recipes in the TV guide, grocery lists on receipts, poems on unpaid bills, love notes to my dad on his newspaper. Sometimes she'd even take the predictable path and write her ideas in a notebook.

Her writings were ordinary, everyday stuff, but sometimes her pen rushed across the page like a mad prospector seeking, sifting for, and striking, gold. She, the first female sessional philosophy lecturer at the University of Toronto, the mad poetess, the wife and mother of two, not to mention diagnosed bipolar [i.e., having bipolar disorder, or manic depression], dwelling mainly in mania—was enviously prolific.

From quantity comes quality, she strongly believed. "That's how I found your dad,"—her second husband—she'd tell me. "It was the Sixties, sure, but you wouldn't believe how many men I had to go through to get to him."

Studying and Finding Meaning in the List

After I discovered the list, dad and I went on to analyze my finding as carefully as if it were a piece of the Dead Sea Scrolls. We decided the list was probably penned some time in the last year of mom's life—amid pain and intensive-care-unit visits and dodgeball games with death. It seemed instructional, a reminder to her that, though she may have been dying, there were still some pretty good reasons to remember that she wasn't gone yet.

We joked about the rankings: dad got No. 4, my brother and I, No. 5. Yet I don't know if the order held any real meaning. It may have come out in one caffeinated burst at 3 a.m., like so much of her work. Maybe it wasn't complete and there's a page 2 out there somewhere. I'm sure it was reflective of what was going on with her when she wrote it. She was pretty angry with her God, in those days; otherwise I'm positive He'd be right up there, outranking us all.

This list wasn't so precious simply because I'd found something she'd written, something she'd touched, though I was still in the unexpected "my mother, the saint, let's build a shrine" stage of grief.

It was because I'd found something very personal to her that also became crucial to me, at a critical juncture in my grief. For her, the list may have been life-sustaining, but for me, it might have been life-saving.

I was amazed at how wonderfully the words transcended her life and death, then, now, and probably 50 years from now. When I found it, I was struggling, feeling unmoored and unhinged and scared of the world. The list offered me something to hold onto. Maybe it did the same for her.

The list is pretty universal: love, humanity, passion, philosophy, knowledge and beauty, life and death. It has headings and subheadings and explanations under each. She was a big thinker and, despite the drugs, remained pretty lucid until the day she slid into that languorous pre-death coma.

If I were to make such a list myself, many of the main topics would be similar. The difference, of course, would be in the details. This makes me realize how much we were alike concerning things that, at the end of our days, really matter.

Using the List in My Life

To this day, I use her gift. I photocopied it and carry it in my wallet, and I suck strength and life and comfort and wisdom out of its never-ending supply.

The words and their vast depth of meaning are at my fingertips. So, then, is my mother's spirit.

Sometimes, if I'm having a "woman on the verge of a nervous breakdown" moment, I'll key in on one item from the now-memorized list and walk around with it, keeping my mind alert and present for clues that might fill in pieces of a bigger puzzle. This encourages me to live in awe, to look, to learn and to see things from new angles, which is not a bad way to spend time.

And my own list? Well, I keep it in the computer upstairs, mentally revising and re-ordering as time goes on. And maybe, one day, I'll write it down on a napkin, tuck it away and let destiny flutter off with it.

Saying Goodbye to a Beloved Aunt

Robin Stratton

Robin Stratton has been a nun for over forty years and has writ-ten and published articles on various spiritual topics. In this piece she describes some of her favorite memories of her recently deceased Aunt Bib. Aunt Bib loved and mothered many children in the family, although she never married and had no children herself. After being told the funeral will be a closed-casket service, Stratton describes her need to see her aunt again and say good-bye in person. She arrives at the funeral parlor early to have a few moments with her aunt where she finds some closure in kiss-ing her cheek and telling her she loves her one last time.

M y cousin telephoned to say Aunt Bib is dead. The funeral is two days hence. No need to wait; at 94 she has outlived all her peers. The pastor will officiate. Of course, I reply. Will you sing, she asks? Of course. And you'll come back to the house afterward? Of course. It will be good to have everyone together again. It will. Good-bye. Good-bye.

The following morning she calls again. The organist will meet you at church an hour before Mass. That will be fine. The family will gather at the funeral parlor to pray the Rosary. Fine. There will be no viewing. Ohhhh. We'll see you tomor-row. I lay the telephone in its cradle. No viewing . . . never see her again . . . never say good-bye. But I must. I must.

Aunt Bib's name was Elisabeth—spelled with an "s," she would explain. Her sisters used that name, as did her friends of many years. To her acquaintances she was Miss d'Invilliers; but to the younger generations of nieces and nephews, she was always Aunt Bib or Aunt Bibby. I don't know who started "Bibby-darling," but it was a commonly accepted term of endearment once she was middle-aged.

A Final Visit

It is a two-hour drive to Philadelphia. I go directly to the funeral parlor, ring the bell and wait. A long minute passes before the lock turns and the heavy door opens. A portly, dark-suited gentleman, his face awash with funereal solemnity, addresses me: "Yes?" I ask to visit Miss d'Invilliers' body. It sounds so cold, so clinical. After all, I cannot tell him she dried my tears, listened to my secrets, told me stories and prayed for me for 50 years. He hesitates. "There are no flowers in the room." "Silly man," I want to say, "I didn't come to see the flowers. I only want to be with Bibby-darling one more time." But instead I say, "That's quite all right."

He ushers me inside: "Please wait." He melts into the thick, dark velvet drapes and disappears. I hear him shuffle about, his heavy footsteps deadened by the carpeting. A dim, rose-colored ray of light slips between the drape and doorframe. Then he reappears and holds the drape aside: "You may go in." The drape falls silently behind me.

My heart drags behind my feet as I approach the open casket. Bibby was always tiny; now, wasted by months of dying, she is as small as a child. I loom over her like some great giant. I kneel. It brings her closer. My eyes are drawn to her hands. The large diamond is missing; her finger looks strangely bare. I once asked about the ring. It had belonged to a woman she nursed many years ago. "She had no way to pay me, so she gave me the ring before she died. I couldn't bear to sell it." Though she could have used the money, Bibby wore the ring for 40 years. What has happened to it, I wonder, as I rest my large hand on her tiny wrinkled ones.

My attention shifts to her face, and I realize her eyes will never again invite me into my heart-space. Those wonderful warm brown eyes, wide with wonder and soft with compassion, dancing with laughter and brimming with tears. Bibby's heart hung in the windows of her eyes.

Memories of Aunt Bib

Her house smelled of newly scrubbed floors and freshly baked cookies. When I was three or four, we would lie on the floor together as Aunt Bibby built cardhouses with infinite patience, all the while warning me not to breathe lest the house come tumbling down. Excitement mounted until the last card was in place. Then we would both take a deep breath, and blow the house down amid shrieks of laughter.

Aunt Bib never read to me. She preferred to tell stories— stories of the family, of the French several greats-grandmother who sent her two little boys to America, of aunts and uncles and cousins who peopled her childhood. She told unforgettable stories, making them up on a moment's notice: stories of bad brownies who lived in the cellar and of children who got lost in the woods. But when she gathered a stuffed animal in her arms, I was ready for the best treat of all. Dogs and teddy bears came alive as we paraded out of the house, Aunt Bib in the lead. We marched into the woods or around the neighborhood, wherever the plot led us. When I was very little, I marveled that the story always ended "happily ever after" the very moment we turned the door knob to reenter her house.

How will the next generation of babies grow up without a Bibby-darling? Who will tell the stories? Even as I ask the question, I realize the answer is contained in the genealogy we pored over last month when we celebrated the birth of the newest child to bear the family name. Aunt Bib herself inherited the story—and perhaps the storytelling as well—and spent her life handing it on to us for safekeeping. She is the last of her generation. We all now move up a notch to assume more responsibility for handing on the faith and sense of family she entrusted to us. Tonight and tomorrow and in the days to come it will be our turn to tell the stories.

Final Rituals

I kneel uncomfortably. . . . What a great lover she was. Four generations of children cuddled in her lap, rocked in her arms, dandled on her knees. Four generations of adults confided in her. Though she never married, she mothered us all. As a young woman, she had wanted to enter the convent. When the mother superior told her she was needed at home, she said no more about becoming a nun. She simply lived her vows as daughter, sister, aunt, friend and confidante for 60 years.

At the age of 82, she was received into the Secular Order of Saint Francis, taking the name Regina. As Sister Regina, Bibby radiated new depths of inner joy that God had allowed her to be a "sister" these few years. We had a long conversation several years ago. She confided to me she didn't think it would be difficult to die. After all, she said, it was simply a matter of moving from one world to another. I hope it was. And I hope heaven is all the love she lavished on others returned a thousandfold to her.

I rise, bend over and kiss her cheek, pat her hand and tell her I love her. Lifelong rituals, one last time. "She was a very special person in our family," I remark as the funeral director ushers me to the door. "That's nice," he replies, closing the heavy door behind me.

A Father's Grief

Howard Twitty

Howard Twitty has been a professional golfer since 1974 and began playing on the Professional Golf Association Tour in 1999. Twitty, his wife, and six children live in Scottsdale, Arizona. This piece is an account of Twitty's thoughts and emotions after losing his son Kevin in a swimming pool accident. Twitty describes some fond memories of his son, including times when Kevin caddied for him on the professional tour. He also describes how difficult it is to continue playing professional golf in the midst of his grief, especially seeing other father-and-son teams on the golf course. Twitty focuses his attention on his remaining children as a way of coping with his grief.

We pulled up alongside each other by accident one afternoon last March [2002], while we were driving down Glendale Road in Phoenix. I can't recall exactly what we said to each other across lanes, but I do remember the sense of excitement in my son's voice. Finally, after years of drifting, Kevin had a plan for the future. He was going to real estate school. He was in love. What more could a father want? That was the last time I saw him. A few days later, on March 23, he was gone, having drowned in a pool at his friend's apartment complex. Kevin was 25.

More than a year has passed, and I think of Kevin many times every day—on and off the course. Everything has changed.

I've gone through all the standard emotions. Denial was a big one. For months I would wake up every morning and feel as if Kevin's death was some horrible dream, and then it would hit me all over again: He is dead. It was not a dream.

I try not to ponder the unknowable: Had he been out in the sun too long that day? He and a friend had gone on an hourlong hike up Squaw Peak in the early afternoon, when the temperature was close to 100. Did he drink enough water? After the hike they went to a bar and had a few beers. Did he have one too many? The answers won't bring him back. I never went to the pool. What good would that do? It is better to think about Kevin's life, not his death.

Spending Time Together on the Golf Course

The two of us weren't always as close as we could've been. His mother and I divorced when he was a teenager, and for many years he blamed me. It wasn't until a full decade later, in 1999, when he caddied for me on the Senior tour, that we spent a lot of quality time together. Was I trying to make up for lost opportunities? You bet. Thank God I did. He behaved perfectly on the course, but the greater rewards came outside the ropes. He entertained me so much with his stories about his buddies and their adventures.

One night, after caddying for me in Montreal [Canada], Kevin and Michael Zarley, [pro golfer] Kermit's son, borrowed a courtesy car to go out looking for a good time. The next morning, when he got up to take a shower, I noticed all these phone numbers on his arm. He told me they had crashed a bachelorette party, and he produced some little pieces of paper with even more numbers. It was all a game to him to see how many fish he could get on the line. He was into the catch-and-release program. He never called any of the girls. Every time I see a pretty girl now, I think of Kevin and wonder if he'd get her number.

After about 15 tournaments, though, I told Kevin that it was time for him to move on. Being a professional caddie was not going to be his life. Besides, I didn't want to be a crutch for him. I could tell he was a little hurt, but he knew I was right.

I think a lot about our days on tour together, which can be a real problem when I'm paired with another player who has his son on the bag. Last year [2002], in Winston-Salem, N.C., I played extremely well in the first round. The next day my threesome included Larry Nelson, whose son Drew was caddying for him. Kevin and Drew had gone way back, from the time they hung out together in the regular Tour's nursery. I hit the ball horribly. My mind went in so many different directions. I thought playing alongside Drew might be difficult, but I had no idea how difficult. I didn't want Larry to feel bad. It wasn't his fault.

Difficulty Returning to Golf

I had a lot of rounds like that [that] year. I simply didn't care. At the Tradition, the first tournament I entered after Kevin died, I was put on the clock for slow play. I didn't swear at the official, but it's safe to say that I wasn't very respectful, either. My colleagues on the tour were great in the beginning, saying the right things, asking me to dinner to make sure I wouldn't be alone. I will always appreciate that. Of course, for them, the whole thing lasted a few weeks, maybe months. Then it was over. For me, it will never be over. Now when they ask how things are going, I know they mean well, but I can tell by their body language that they don't want a long conversation about it. I don't blame them. It's not fair for me to place my baggage on their carts. We're out there competing against one another. We're not there to console one another.

Sometimes people, even though they have the most well-meaning intentions, can say things that a grieving parent doesn't want to hear, such as, "I know how you feel." I want to shout back, "No, you don't." Another one is, "Be thankful that you have six other kids." I am, but that doesn't lessen the loss of Kevin. Some tell me that "he's in a better place." Better place? A better place would be on this earth with me and his family, to live his life. And then, finally, there's the one that troubles me the most, "It was God's will." I'm sorry, but while I suppose it is true that God takes 25-year-old sons, I'm still having trouble trying to work through why.

August [2002] was a turning point. My wife, Sheree, helped me recognize that I wasn't grieving for Kevin; I was grieving for myself. Worse yet, that was taking my attention away from our six other kids (ages 6 to 22). I know that Kevin wouldn't want that, and that if he could write me a letter, he would tell me to be sad that he's gone but not to destroy my life or ignore the people he loved. I think about that a lot. Losing him, I hope, has made me a better father. I make sure to go to my kids' soccer games, to help with their homework, to do all the things I won't have a chance to do with Kevin.

Losing More than a Son

I didn't lose only Kevin. I also lost Michelle, the wonderful girl he was planning to marry. (That's what he told his mother only weeks before he died.) I knew this relationship was different the day Kevin said he had a girl he wanted me to meet. He had never done that before. This was one number he didn't throw away. I've spoken to her on the phone a few times since Kevin's death, but it's always awkward. What do we say to each other? Where can we possibly go from here?

I've also lost Kevin's friends. I wonder how they're coping. On the night of his funeral a bunch of them went to this dive in Phoenix. The drinks were on Kevin—he'd been working for the Arizona Department of Transportation, and his last paycheck had just arrived in the mail. Everyone told Kevin stories, like the one about how he got kicked out of a bar for fighting with some guy whose girlfriend he had been flirting with. The tab got to be about $1,300. It was fun seeing all his friends together, though painful to see them cry. Nobody wanted the night to end. Kevin would've had such a great time. He was always the life of the party.

I worry most about his sister, Jocelyn. She's 22 and doesn't say much, so I'm not quite sure how she's doing. Kevin and Jocelyn were incredibly close. Right now all I can do is wait until she's ready, but I'll be there for her when she is.

A Parent's Perspective on Grief

People say losing a child is the worst. I know of nothing more accurate. It's like joining a club you don't want to belong to— and you're in it for life. At the [2002] Senior Players Championship a man came up to me after I'd finished my round and explained how he had lost his daughter. Suddenly, this complete stranger and I had a bond that is impossible to describe, unless you belong to the club. We each knew exactly what the other was feeling.

I try to think of the other parents out there who have gone through this experience, and I have no magical words. It's impossible to explain to someone who has never lost a child, sort of like trying to describe the color blue to a blind person. All I can tell others is that it's O.K. to remember. In fact, it's imperative. Yes, I lost Kevin, but I still have the memory.

I've lost my share of loved ones. I had an older brother, an electrician, who died when he touched the wrong wire and a sister who was taken by cancer. While I certainly experienced my share of grieving, there was no way I could truly understand what my mother must have been going through. I think I do now and, as a result, have such tremendous respect for how she has coped. At 92 she remains an inspiration to a son who still counts on her guidance.

Coping with Grief

Since Kevin died, I have found myself looking at the [obituaries] in the newspaper every day, searching for the names and stories of young people. Why? I'm not really sure. I suppose because it's a kind of therapy, a way to connect with Kevin.

I do connect with him in many ways. One is the Sarah Brightman CD *Time to Say Goodbye*. I play the title song over and over. He loved it so much.

Another connection is the Chapstick I keep in my pocket. I got the idea in August after a conversation with a friend who had lost her son. She explained the importance of finding a physical object to represent the lost child. Chapstick was the obvious choice for me. It was a family joke that Kevin always tried to carry one and would even use other people's. I know it sounds hokey, but when I use the Chapstick, it's like I'm giving him a kiss. When I used up a stick at a tournament in Hawaii [in 2002], I didn't know what to do with the empty container. I couldn't simply throw it in the garbage.

I decided to dig a little hole overlooking a beautiful cove and buried the container in it. I knew Kevin would like it there.

Cherishing a Fatally Ill Infant

Amy Kuebelbeck

Amy Kuebelbeck is a mother and former reporter and editor for the Associated Press and several major newspapers. She lives in St. Paul, Minnesota, with her husband and two daughters. The following narrative details Kuebelbeck's experience of receiving a prenatal diagnosis of a lethal heart condition in the male fetus she was carrying. Rather than terminating the pregnancy, Kuebelbeck and her husband decided to use the rest of the pregnancy to cherish their son's life. Kuebelbeck describes the joys and sorrows of the remainder of the pregnancy and how she and her family dealt with the birth and loss of Gabriel.

"You have a beautiful baby," the ultrasound technician said quietly. She was studying the flickering images on her screen, staring intently at the shadows of the tiny heart. I think she had already seen that our baby was going to die.

After two routine but inconclusive ultrasounds elsewhere, I had been referred to United Hospital in St. Paul for a better look at our baby's heart. So after an agonizing week of waiting, my husband and I found ourselves in a darkened exam room, trying to believe the baby was fine, trying not to panic.

The rhythmic whooshing seemed to fill the room, a reassuring sound in other circumstances. She fell silent. Looking, pressing on my belly to try to nudge the baby into another position, tapping keys on the machine's keyboard. Looking. Was that the sound of my baby's heart or mine? Finally, I ventured, "For telling our families—does it look like something is wrong?" She kept her eyes on the screen and said quietly, "Yes."

Getting the Diagnosis

Clutching wet Kleenex and each other, Mark and I waited while the technician left to get a perinatologist, a specialist in high-risk pregnancies. The perinatologist came in and matter-of-factly explained that the baby had a severe heart problem that was incurable and fatal. Fatal. Our baby. She said the pregnancy likely would continue normally and the baby would be fine until he or she was born. Then we would have three options. We could try an aggressive and risky series of three open-heart surgeries, beginning with a procedure called the Norwood, which would not be a cure but could possibly keep our baby alive indefinitely. We could try a heart transplant, but the odds of finding an infant donor in time would be small. Or we could provide comfort care, keeping the baby comfortable until death came naturally, probably within a few days.

Choked by tears, we asked if our baby would die peacefully if we decided on comfort care. She said yes. We had one more question. Was our baby a boy or a girl? The ultrasound technician said she thought the baby looked like a boy. She gave us a printout, an otherworldly profile of his little face.

Back at home, I brushed past the babysitter and headed straight for our girls. I needed to hold a child of mine in my arms, even if it wasn't our new baby. The girls were only four and two, but they could tell something was wrong. Mark came in, and we all sat on the couch together, Mark holding Elena, and Maria sharing my lap with the baby, who was kicking contentedly inside of me.

"The baby has a sick heart," Mark began, before starting to cry.

The Decision

Two of the most primal parental instincts are to keep your child alive and to protect your child from unnecessary pain. Those instincts usually do not collide.

With our baby, they did.

When modern medicine can offer even the remotest hope of a cure, the decision to try seems easy. Suddenly things that once seemed so terrible—the machines, the cutting through bone and flesh, even the experimental treatments—appear to offer a potential, though terrifying, lifeline up from the abyss. But what do you do when none of the options offers hope of reasonable success?

We were referred to a pediatric cardiologist for more tests. During one of our lengthy visits with him, we asked him the question that probably no doctor wants to hear but is impossible for parents not to ask: What would you do if this were your baby? He said carefully, "I've seen a lot of babies suffer unnecessarily."

He explained that even babies who survive one or more of the reconstructive surgeries face a real risk of grave complications, including strokes and brain damage from the lack of oxygen. The doctor also mentioned that his wife was a pediatric intensivist, a specialist whose life's work was treating critically ill children. Unlike us, she would not be queasy about surgery or feeding tubes or machines. She would have an acute sense of the miracles medicine could effect—and also of its limits. He said that after watching so many babies with this condition struggle in vain, she felt strongly that she would not intervene.

In the weeks and months to come, we would think of that answer again and again. . . .

Getting the Spiritual Perspective

We also needed to talk with an expert of another realm.

We found ourselves sitting in the office of Father Bill Baer, then-pastor of Nativity of Our Lord Church in St. Paul, who, we quickly learned, knew a great deal about our baby's condition.

I told him that the main reason we came to talk with him was that we wanted to know if the church would consider surgical intervention in our baby's case to be "extraordinary means." While the Catholic Church strives to be a strong voice in defense of life, the church also teaches that one is not obligated to undertake extraordinary medical means in order to sustain life. The church also draws a sharp ethical line between withholding extraordinary treatment, thus allowing death to come naturally, and taking direct actions intended to end a life. You might say that the church does not insist on artificially maintaining life at all costs, but it does insist on reverence for life at all costs.

Slicing open the chest, sawing through the breast-bone. Three times. All for no cure.

"It just seems like too much to ask of a baby," I said tearfully.

Father Baer seemed to draw himself up a bit taller in his chair. "I can tell you, as Christ's representative to you on this earth," he began, "that you have no moral obligation to operate."

Choosing a Peaceful Death for Gabriel

As we waded through all the statistics about survival rates, percentages of this and risks of that, we began to focus on other statistics that were unspoken. It became increasingly clear to us that even with surgeries—assuming our baby lived through them in the first place—his chances of getting a normally functioning, reliable heart were zero. His chances of unimaginable pain and a lifetime of uncertainty: 100 percent.

Call it pessimism or lack of faith in doctors or lack of faith in God, but we also did not believe that he would survive the surgeries. It seemed to us that the . . . choice we were being asked to make on behalf of our son was not between life and death but between a painful death and a peaceful one. So with broken hearts of our own, we decided to forgo medical intervention for our beautiful baby and his imperfect heart.

In our view, comfort care did not mean that we would do nothing. We felt we would be parenting him in another profound way: we would be protecting him from the medical onslaught.

Our doctors and nurses, especially the nurses, understood. One told us that she thought we would find peace in knowing that we were sparing our baby from being turned into a "science experiment." Said another, kindly and with tears in her eyes, "You're going to love him to death."

No one could give Gabriel—which is what we decided to name him—a good heart, So we set out to give him a good life.

Waiting with Gabriel

How was I supposed to walk around pregnant for three and a half more months, knowing Our baby was going to die? How could I even go to the grocery store and have a cashier ask casually when my baby was due?

But even though I was the one walking around pregnant, I also was favored with constant reminders that Gabriel was still alive and safe inside of me. No matter where I went, I could take him with me. And when the grief came crashing over me, I could seek solace in curling around him. Among all the people being affected by Gabriel's expected death, I began to feel like the fortunate one.

In my ravenous search for information, I returned again and again to a website for parents who continued their pregnancies after receiving a devastating fatal diagnosis. The site was titled "Waiting with Love."

Waiting with love.

It gave us words for exactly what we wanted to do.

I devoured newsletters and books from the Pregnancy and Infant Loss Center, a trailblazing group in Wayzata

[Minnesota] that has since been folded into other organizations. Through tears, I looked at birth-death announcement cards in a catalog from A Place to Remember, a St. Paul company that sells materials for people facing a crisis in pregnancy or infant death. Particularly heartbreaking was a photograph in the booklet *When Hello Means Goodbye* of a couple tenderly dressing their stillborn son. Visible in the photograph was the baby's tiny hand, perfect and limp.

Other parents' stories helped foreshadow what might happen to us and gave us ideas for honoring Gabriel's short life. The stories helped light our path. And they showed us it was possible to make it through to the other side. . . .

There is no good era in which to lose a child, although times in the past have been much worse.

Tragically, infant death often was, and in too many places still is, greatly minimized. Especially once childbirth became the province of hospitals, by the 1940s and 1950s. Stillborn babies and babies who died shortly after birth often were whisked away while their mothers were still sedated and exhausted from childbirth. Even in the 1980s, many hospitals still prohibited parents from seeing or holding their stillborn babies. Parents were told to simply forget about that baby and have another one, as if children were interchangeable. Parents were made to feel that naming the baby was morbid and unnecessary. Discussing infant death became taboo.

The infant mortality rate has dropped considerably in the United States since the early 1900s, when an estimated 10 percent of all babies died before their first birthday. The rate is now less than 1 percent. But that still represents a lot of babies, and a lot of grieving parents. About twenty-eight thousand infants a year die before their first birthday, and about a million U.S. pregnancies end in miscarriage or stillbirth every year.

In part because of the loving work of parents whose profound loss was minimized or ignored in the past, many newly bereaved parents are now encouraged to hold their child's body, to give their baby a name, and to take photographs of their baby. Nurses help parents collect priceless mementos such as handprints, footprints, and a lock of hair. Parents are encouraged to hold a memorial service of some kind and to wait until the mother is physically able to attend.

These parents will not be leaving the hospital with a baby, but, unlike far too many heartbroken mothers and fathers in the past, they will at least be recognized as parents of a unique, irreplaceable child.

A Cocoon of Goodness

We lived in a strange twilight of grief while we waited for Gabriel to be born, as many families do during the last stages of a family member's fatal illness. Many wonderful people were willing to wait in that twilight with us. Our phone rang often, with my mom and five sisters checking in and probably bracing themselves for what would surely be a long, tearful monologue from me. Family and friends invited us over often so all our kids could play and we could talk. People organized prayers on our behalf. Friends who also had lost a baby made it a point to call on Mother's Day; remembering how difficult that day was for them while they were awaiting their daughter's birth and death.

During one of our meetings with Father Baer, he said that people experiencing great sorrow sometimes tell him that, strangely, it gives them glimpses of heaven. He seemed to suggest this carefully, as though he was bracing himself for a potentially explosive response. Heaven? What kind of ivory tower do you live in? My baby is going to die. This isn't heaven; this is pure hell. If someone had insensitively suggested this to us too soon after the diagnosis, that might have been our reaction. But we understood what he meant. We were already overwhelmed and humbled by the cumulative effect of people's gestures of love and support. Strand by strand, we were being enveloped in—to borrow a phrase from novelist Jon Hassler—"a cocoon of goodness."

Spending the Summer with Gabriel

We tried to give our girls, and ourselves, as normal a summer as possible. Many times we spoke of doing something "with Gabriel." We took him fishing on a secluded lake near Ely, [Minnesota,] where Mark was teaching a summer environmental studies course. I took Gabriel swinging on the girls' backyard swings. We took him to a Minnesota Twins game at the Metrodome (Mark's idea) and to a concert by the male vocal ensemble Chanticleer at Orchestra Hall (mine). I had returned to my editing job at The Associated Press two weeks after the diagnosis, but my wonderfully understanding supervisors made it possible for me to step away eight weeks before the due date, giving us priceless time to spend our bittersweet summer as a complete family.

An obvious pregnancy is as natural a topic for small talk as the weather. "When's your baby due?" "Do you know if you're having a boy or a girl?" Of course we got those questions too. We decided generally that if the questioner were someone we would need to see again, we would relate a brief version of the story. Other times we tried to accept people's congratulations graciously. In a way, it was nice to have people acknowledge our baby without their comments being tinged with sympathy. . . .

Everything was ready. My hospital bag was packed. All our preparations had been made for Gabriel's birth—and for his death. I wondered what he looked like and what his days would be like with us at home. Does he look like his sisters? What will he sound like when he cries? I yearned to feel his soft cheek against mine, to feel his swaddled weight against my chest, to cup the back of his head in my hand, to breathe deeply of his sweet baby smell. To try to imprint everything of him on my memory forever.

I was ready to meet my son. . . .

Gabriel's Birth

One more push. A tremendous, searing, unstoppable rush. At 4:42 p.m., Gabriel is born. He is on my chest, crying weakly, wet and warm and alive.

"Hello, Gabriel, I'm your mommy," I say into his ear. "I'm so glad you're here."

Mark cuts the umbilical cord, and the neonatology team sweeps Gabriel to the nearby warmer to try to suction the meconium—too, too much—from his lungs.

Breathe, sweetheart. Cough that up.

"Don't you want us to do anything else?" someone on the neonatology team asks.

For a microsecond, my thoughts leap. Is there something else? Some new treatment we don't know about?

We shake our heads no.

At last we are holding our beautiful baby.

Swaddled in his hospital blanket decorated with pastel teddy bears and hot-air balloons, he is crying with some effort, his eyes squeezed tightly closed. He has the plump newborn cheeks his sisters had and a hint of downy dark hair. He is a little pale, and his fingernails are faintly blue. He is beautiful.

Mark helps unwrap him for the measurement—seven pounds, nine ounces; twenty-two inches long. Gabriel does not like this one bit. He wails, his mouth wide open in protest. Then he is swaddled again in my arms and the waiting room empties into our room. There are tears and smiles and camera flashes. He is beautiful, cream-skinned and perfect and plump, with no bruises or misshapen head from the delivery. My parents hold him briefly, then give me a baptism gift, a gold necklace pendant of a mother and child. Mom helps me put it on.

Gabriel's Death

The pediatric cardiologist, who has begun examining Gabriel, says his heart condition is among the severest cases she has seen.

We ask if the exam gives any indication of how long he will live. No, she says; he could live for up to two weeks. My mom starts mentally calculating how to schedule people in shifts to help us at home for that long.

It is just the three of us now, Mark and I and our son. I kiss Gabriel's forehead. It is cool.

The nurse comes back and checks his temperature and his heart. His heart rate is only 67 beats per minute, much slower than the normal newborn rate of 100 to 120 beats a minute. She slips out of the room.

I kiss him again and whisper to him, "Don't leave yet."

The nurse comes back and listens with her stethoscope again. "Six," she said.

Six? We don't understand.

Her face close to mine, she says gently, "Your baby is dying."

No! Not yet!

The words scream through my mind, but nothing comes out except a sob.

My family streams into the room. All our faces are wet with tears.

"I thought we were going to be able to keep him longer," I say helplessly. I wanted the girls to hold him. I wanted to nurse him. I wanted to bring him home.

Someone mentions the priest.

"You don't have time," the nurse says urgently. "You realize that anybody can baptize a baby, right?"

Yes, we know.

Mark touches Gabriel's forehead with a drop of water, making the sign of the cross. "I baptize you in the name of the Father, the Son, and the Holy Spirit," he says, his voice thick with crying.

Gabriel is in my lap. Mark and I are cradling his head and his cheek, and Mark's arm is around me. Gabriel's eyes are closed. He appears to be sleeping peacefully. Oh, sweetheart, I never even saw your eyes. "Let's look at him," I whisper. We open the blanket and see his arms resting on his chest, his knees pulled up as though he were still in the womb, those tiny feet that kicked me for months. Everything about him seems perfect. We wrap him up again. My hands cradle his bare head and cup his shoulder. Mark holds Gabriel's left hand, and Gabriel's fingers grip Mark's little finger.

We are surrounded by people who love him. Like holding a vigil for a baby about to be born, all of us simply wait together, waiting with Gabriel. The only sounds are of people crying softly. Gabriel is in the same bed where he had been born, the sheets still bloodstained from his birth. We watch as he takes small, infrequent breaths, and finally his imperfect little heart stops beating altogether.

Gabriel relaxes his hold on Mark's finger. Mark looks at the clock. It is 7:10 p.m., two and a half hours since Gabriel's first breath. . . .

Saying Goodbye

Mark and I took turns holding him and rocking him in the rocking chair. We finally called the nurses' station to say that we were ready for someone to take him away. We laid him in a hospital blanket in the nurse's arms. She walked past the curtain and out the door, taking with her our baby and a part of us.

I was strangely eager for the wake; I could hardly wait to see Gabriel again and to hold him one final time. I knew that I needed to hold his body again. I am forever grateful that I did, but not for the reasons I expected. Holding his body gave me final, irrefutable proof that Gabriel was no longer in that shell. It felt like a doll, stiff and hollow and light. It didn't smell like him. It didn't even really look like him. It wasn't him. He didn't need it anymore, so we didn't either.

It might seem counterintuitive, but holding that empty body for just a few moments made it much easier to release it and to close the red cedar lid of that small casket forever.

At the cemetery, the sky threatened rain, the wind rippling the girls' dresses. As people started to drift away after the graveside prayers, Mark, holding Maria with one arm, stepped closer to the casket. He reached out and touched the polished lid one last time, a final benediction from father to son.

Confirmation of the Decision to Provide Comfort Care

At first we felt profoundly cheated that Gabriel did not live long enough to come home with us. This eventually dissolved into a sense of relief and gratitude. We now think of Gabriel's leaving so soon as one of his many gifts to us.

He was so sick that he would have been a terrible candidate for surgery. So after all those months of researching and agonizing and lying awake in the middle of the night, we had proof that we had chosen the right path for him. We ached to have him in our arms longer, but the very briefness of his visit released us forever from second thoughts about whether we should have operated.

Maybe the circumstances of his birth and death were our miracle. We could not have choreographed it any better. Gabriel spent his entire life literally surrounded by people who loved him. He died peacefully and painlessly in his parents' arms. If he had to leave us, it was a beautiful way to go.

Knowing ahead of time about Gabriel's heart condition meant that our precious hours with him once he was born were not filled with that initial shock and grief and confusion. He never left the room where he was born; he never left my sight. If we had not known about his heart, our caregivers would surely have swept him away from me in a desperate effort to figure out what was so terribly wrong. If we had not known, I might never have held my son in my arms while he was alive.

As we wrote to our pediatric cardiologist after Gabriel died, doctors probably consider the death of an infant to be a medical failure. But, in a way, we view what happened as a medical success. Doctors' expertise in diagnosing the condition and their candor in advising us about the treatment options helped us give Gabriel a good, although brief, life. And a good death.

Confirmation of the Decision to Wait with Gabriel

People sometimes are astonished—and perhaps a little horrified—that I walked around for three and a half months carrying a baby I knew would die.

We knew we could have aborted the pregnancy legally. But now that we've been through it, I believe ending our pregnancy early would have been disastrous on many levels. It would have meant denying ourselves the life-changing, bittersweet, exquisite experience of holding our beautiful full-term son and hearing his cries. Ending the pregnancy early would have meant rejecting a gift.

It would not have been a shortcut through our grief. If anything, our grief would have been magnified.

Perhaps some people thought we were bringing grief upon ourselves by continuing the pregnancy and later having a full funeral and burial. They might have thought that we should just get on with our lives. But for that brief time, Gabriel was our life. Other than caring for our girls, there was nothing more important than waiting with Gabriel, giving him the full measure of our time and attention and love.

Yes, Gabriel was going to die. But first he was going to live.

CHAPTER 2

The Role of Faith in
the Grieving Process

A Stillborn Child Challenges a Mother's Catholic Faith

Anne Donovan

In this piece Anne Donovan describes giving birth to a dead child and the crisis of faith it caused her. Her pain and confusion toward God strains her marriage as her husband looks for comfort and strength in his faith. She questions God's mercy and begins to believe that prayer is useless. After some time passes, Anne Donovan begins to attempt to redefine her relationship with God. She reflects that seeing and holding her perfectly formed daughter, even though she was dead, reinforced for her that God was there. Anne Donovan is a pen name for this mother who grew up in Catholic schools, studied theology, and considers herself a liberal Catholic. She now has a healthy son.

At my nephew's baptism, I sat gripping my angel-locket in a futile attempt to keep from sobbing. My tremors were causing the entire pew to shake, and people were staring, but I could not stop. I studied my husband's hand as he tried to steady my trembling knees. I smoothed my skirt again and again—anything to avoid looking at the gurgling white bundle that was being proudly displayed 10 feet in front of me.

I almost made it through the ceremony. Almost. But when the priest had finished baptizing Joseph, he turned to remind everyone sternly, "Life is a precious gift from God."

Then what did I get? I whispered as I rushed from the church. What did I get?

My nephew Joseph was born a month after I buried my daughter Carly. The morning of Joseph's christening, I sat in the cherry rocking chair I had purchased for her, hoping the gentle motion would lull me into detachment.

John, my husband, crouched in front of me, wearing the same navy suit he'd worn to Carly's funeral. He would never notice a thing like that, I thought. "It's time to go," he said quietly. "We'll be late." He started to pull me up.

"I can't do it." I began to cry, watching milk spread into a stain on my chest.

"Yes, you can." His voice was impatient. We'd been over this several times.

"I don't want to go." . . .

Anger at God

In the end, my attention to loyalty won out and I attended the christening, determined to show Lucy and Frank [John's sister and her husband] that I could move on, or something equally perverse. It was an enormous mistake. Despite my best efforts to behave, I made quite a scene and ended up in the basement of the church, demanding an explanation from God. Why were these hypocrites upstairs—neither of whom ever went to church, hadn't even been married in a church—why were they happily christening their "gift from God," while I sobbed for my dead baby? I'd been a good Catholic, I'd done what I was supposed to, why punish me? John eventually found me, ranting to the dusty furniture. He was humiliated by my inability to control myself and ordered me to pull myself together, go back upstairs and be sociable.

"Where is my husband?" I asked, sickened that he expected me to hide my grief. I left him standing on the concrete steps, yelling at me to stop being so dramatic. The ensuing argument, stretched over weeks, nearly broke us apart. After long sessions in which I tried to find words for what I was feeling, and John's rapid rebuttals, we finally began to understand just how differently Carly's death had affected us. He had become a control freak, leaning heavily on tradition and platitudes, lighting candles in every church he passed, but I had lost faith in rituals and answers.

Rules saved John's sanity, but my experience, like our daughter's life, had fallen between the lines. He admitted that he'd been trying to filter out my anger at God. I was his spiritual bedrock, and the thought that I was losing faith terrified him. Then I understood that I had to wade through my grief alone. I didn't resent him; he needed to have hope in his story. But mine is not a story of redemption, or miraculous grace, or salvation. It is a story of simple pain and profound confusion, and the occasional inadequacy of theology when your heart is broken.

My Catholic Beliefs

I am a product of 18 years of elite Catholic education, dominated by liberal Sacred Heart nuns and logic-hungry Jesuits. I've studied it all: morality, Christology, liberation theology, church history—you name it. I consider myself a thinking person's Catholic, one who has argued for—and often railed against—the tenets of Catholicism. I have spent many hours discussing and defending my faith with Catholics and non-Catholics alike. I even enjoyed a stint working with the poor in the Jesuit Volunteer Corps, a decision that forever launched me, in the eyes of family and friends, outside the realms of normal behavior and into unfathomable liberal Catholicism.

But I have a healthy dose of skepticism, too. My faith has survived personal confrontations with issues that remain sticky for the church, challenges that made me threaten to abandon Catholicism altogether. But somehow, I held on. Each stumbling block forced me to reexamine Catholicism, and I always came back less absolute about hierarchy and man-made rules, but with a greater understanding of how personal faith was for me.

So why didn't any of this specialized knowledge and insight comfort me when my obstetrician took my hand and told me that my daughter was dead? Where was all that intricately woven argument, as I sweated and swore my way through delivering our dead baby? I recall it was with a sort of morbid fascination that I fixated on the crucifix hanging on the wall of the birthing room, almost as if it were mocking me. You thought you had this faith business all figured out, kiddo, didn't ya? You thought it was all squared away. So how are you going to deal with this?

The Baby Stopped Kicking

One minute I was lounging on a Cape Cod beach, savoring my last week of pregnancy, the next it occurred to me that baby hadn't kicked me for a while. Feeling silly for calling with yet another complaint, I tracked my obstetrician down in the middle of surgery; he didn't even wait for me to finish. "Where are you? Come right now. I'm at the hospital." John looked possessed as he cursed and sped past slower cars on the highway; I retched into a plastic bag from time to time as I silently pleaded, Please. When the nurses saw me arrive, they led me into a delivery room and hooked up the monitor. When Dr. Modica came rushing into the room in his scrubs and grabbed the ultrasound machine, I knew. He passed the wand over and over my belly but there was no sound. He couldn't conjure any magic this time. He shook his head at the hovering nurses, who, one by one, turned away and broke down. "I am so sorry," he murmured.

While the rest of the city ate barbecue and watched fireworks explode overhead, I lay in a lavender room staring at an incubator I wouldn't need. Pieces of myself, ideals and hopes, accomplishments and desires, dreams and expectations—it all went sliding off in an avalanche of oblivion. Those things I had relied on—modern science, women's intuition, God's mercy—had failed, and I had nothing to hold on to. Medical staff, family members, my husband—they all shifted around me as I was induced and slowly dissolved into labor. There was nothing anyone could do except help me deliver the baby. When a chaplain forced herself into the room to talk about God, I yelled at a nurse to get her away from me.

Losing my Faith

All my multilayered, carefully constructed faith was stripped away as I focused on one thing: the injustice that our little girl didn't have a chance to take even a single breath. It never occurred to me to pray—not from the moment we first heard the news, not when I was in labor and not a month later as I sat at home sorting through my emotions and preparing for a memorial Mass of the Angels.

Prayer seemed so futile, even unnecessary, like throwing a glass of water on a burning house. I had prayed my entire pregnancy for the baby to be healthy—and she was. Carly was perfect—but she wasn't alive, cooing in my arms. How could I not feel betrayed? My mother, who has attended daily Mass for as long as I can remember, encouraged me to join her, to help ease my mind. As much as I admire the strength of her devotion and the real comfort she receives from the ritual of Mass, I could not face going. It wasn't that I was angry at God. It was, and still is, more a sense that I have to be alone and focused to work through this spiritual crisis. . . .

In the weeks following Carly's death, well-meaning friends and relatives called and sent hundreds of cards and letters offering helpless words of condolence. Most of their efforts said the same thing: "It was God's will." We cannot understand God's will. Those words kept me up at night for months, spinning through my frantic mind, tying me in philosophical knots. I know they were trying to help, but every time the issue of God's will sprang up, I was miserable. It got to the point where I couldn't even numbly smile or nod any more when the phrase inevitably popped up. I just clenched my teeth to keep from saying something I'd regret. I finally decided people didn't know what to say, and so they tossed out "God's will" as a life preserver, hoping we would cling to it. . . .

The God I perceive is a God of love and creation, not of destruction. My God is a force of life and affirmation, one who does not randomly interfere with the rhythms of the world. I can't be comforted by the thought that God decided to teach us all a lesson and plucked Carly away. We received several copies of a saccharine poem that people often use when children die. Its gruesome message is that God looked around heaven and decided it needed some brightening up, so he picked a vivid flower—our daughter, or any child—to cheer the place up. This is not a God I can relate to, but I am sure someone out there finds that idea comforting. . . .

I imagine God to be a caring parent, always there, receptive and loving, but sage enough to understand that in order for us to evolve, we need to feel pain and figure out the answers on our own.

There is a medical explanation for my daughter's death, albeit a cruelly inadequate one, but I am willing to accept it. Somehow the umbilical cord ruptured, a swollen purple kink appeared in an otherwise smooth connection. She might have reached out and grasped the cord in her tiny hand, effectively cutting off her own life. It is not an image I can dwell on for very long before I start looking for distractions. . . .

Dealing with Comments from Others

My cousin argued with me, "Well, maybe it isn't God's will that Carly died, but perhaps it was within his will." I don't know how that can be much different. That assumes God could have prevented Carly's death and spared us this pain, but just didn't want to. It assumes some of us are worthy and others not, an idea that still speaks to some grand, orchestrated scheme in which we are all just pawns.

If I believed that, I would have given up a long time ago.

What worries me about all of this is that I realize only a few people are willing to have a dialogue with me that explores the tangled, dark and frightening mess of our doubts and fears and anger over Carly's death. Many of my friends and family lapse into embarrassed silence when I mention her name, as if I have just told a distasteful joke. I started to notice a distinct difference between most of the letters from our Christian friends and those from our Jewish friends. The letters of Jewish friends expressed a genuine exploration of the sense of injustice and pain that the news of Carly's death stirred in them. They acknowledged their confusion and wished that time would be kind to us. They did not try to placate us with the idea that someday we would understand why this happened. They spoke from the heart, telling us only: "This is unfair, it is so painful, it is so tragic, we are thinking of you." We grew to treasure their honesty and their willingness to explore.

I have been told some remarkable things in the interest of consolation. I've been told to rejoice that my daughter went to heaven unmarked by sin, her soul clean and pure, perfect. That God has a special place reserved for her. I have been told that I should feel privileged: I have my very own baby angel, my own divine connection. To me, these are cartoonish images. They are about as comforting as imagining God as a robed elderly man with a long white beard, floating around on a cloud. These are images used to reassure a child, and they feel frozen in time.

I have also been privy to the dark secrets of three older Catholic women who never grieved for their children until they heard about Carly. In the past, they explained, these things "weren't talked about," and they felt it was inappropriate to question God's will. . . .

All three women were profoundly drugged during delivery and their stillborn children were whisked away before they could see them. They have no idea if their children are buried, or where. They have tightly reined in unspeakable pain for 20 or 30 years. I grieve for them because I had the opportunity to bond with my daughter during and after birth.

Sometimes, from their choice of words, I think people misunderstand. They think having a stillborn baby is like a late miscarriage. When we explain about the funeral home, the burial next to my father, the Mass of the Angels—then they begin to understand what we have lost. Our recovery has been slow and full of ups and downs. Finding out we're expecting a second child rejuvenated us; watching my sister-in-law parade her newborn around like a trophy repeatedly tore us down. Only recently have I felt a desire to attend church again and once again attempt to redefine my relationship with God and our community. Maybe I'm just being superstitious. Maybe attending Mass is subconscious insurance for the life of my new little passenger. Maybe I'm beginning to forgive the inadequacy of my faith and fellow believers in easing our pain. I've always said that being a contemporary Catholic is like being married: You may be fully aware of the faults and problems with the institutional church, but you can't help loving it anyway. So maybe these past months have just been one prolonged argument with God and Catholicism, and now it's time to make up.

Giving Birth to Carly

It didn't matter that she was already gone; we were still a team, Carly and I. When it came time to push, all my fears slipped away, and I was filled with a strange combination of strength and serenity. The physical pain hovered somewhere above me, separate, distant. Any doubt that I couldn't handle this birth simply vanished. I was fully aware that I was delivering a human being, and I was determined to bring her into the world with pride and dignity. It was her debut and final appearance, and the least I could do for her was make it an honorable one.

With one enormous effort, it was all over. I struggled to see. Dr. Modica sighed as he pulled Carly to his bloodied smock. "She is beautiful." I fell back on the bed and absorbed the silence. No cries, no gurgles, just the small sounds of my husband's grief. The nurse gently cleaned and swaddled her before approaching me. "Would you like to see your daughter?" she asked, with a smile that made me realize I did want to see her, desperately.

I looked to John, but he was so relieved I was all right that he could only sob into my neck. I didn't hesitate; I had waited so long. As I gathered Carly in my arms, and peeked at her peaceful face, I felt no different from any other new mother. She was still warm from my body, and for a moment I felt she might open her eyes. I brushed my lips against her forehead and John managed to look up. "Hello, sweetheart," he whispered, touching a finger to her white blonde wisps. "You look just like your mommy."

We kept Carly with us for a while, talking some, telling her how much we had wanted her, but mostly we were quiet. We unwrapped the blanket and examined every inch of her, memorizing her tiny toes and the pink tint of her fingernails. But soon, too soon, she grew cold, and our hearts felt so full. No matter how long I held her, nothing would change.

There is an excerpt from a letter Harriet Beecher Stowe wrote to a friend that eloquently captures the essence of my struggle: "When the heartstrings are suddenly cut, it is, I believe, a physical impossibility to feel faith or resignation; there is a revolt of the instinctive and animal system, and though we may submit to God, it is rather by constant painful effort than sweet attraction." Some may wonder why, after our experience, I still want to make the painful effort to believe. I can only respond that, despite my doubts, having seen the breathtaking perfection of my daughter's peaceful face, it is impossible to think God was not there.

Finding God's Grace Through Loss

Gerald L. Sittser

Gerald L. Sittser has a master's degree in divinity and a doctoral degree in the history of Christianity and teaches in the theology department at Whitworth College in Spokane, Washington. He is the father of four children. After the loss of his wife, mother, and daughter in a car accident, Sittser was left to consider the ideas of justice, fairness, and getting what one deserves. He questions why this tragedy happened to him. He concludes that many people have a much better life than they truly deserve and that people should not expect to be exempt from experiencing difficult times. Although the loss of his loved ones has taught him that life is not fair, it has also helped him to experience the grace of God in his life.

I received many cards and letters after the car accident that took the lives of my wife, my four-year-old daughter and my mother. I am grateful that few people presumed to give advice. Instead, they expressed shock, anger and doubt. "Why you?" they kept asking. As one person commented, "Your family appeared so ideal. This tragedy is a terrible injustice. If it can happen to you, it can happen to any of us. Now no one is safe!"

No one is safe, because the universe is hardly a safe place. It is often mean, unpredictable and unjust. Loss has little to do with our notions of fairness. Some people live long and happily, though they deserve to suffer. Others endure one loss after another, though they deserve to be blessed. Loss is no more a respecter of persons and position than good fortune is. There is often no rhyme or reason to the misery of some and to the happiness of others.

Two weeks before the accident Lynda and I fell into a long conversation about what we would do if one of us were to die. We talked about how we would raise the children and what we would find most difficult about being single parents. We wondered which of our friends would remain loyal and which would drift away. We discussed money and time and home maintenance. The subject of remarriage came up, too. We both agreed that under ideal conditions, having two parents in the home is best. But conditions are rarely ideal, which made us cautious about assuming we could find another spouse.

We decided it would be better to remain single and pour energy into the children than to get involved in a relationship that would siphon energy from the home. Then Lynda cracked, "Besides, according to what I know about statistics, there would be no eligible men available to marry me. And according to what I know about you, there would be no women crazy enough to marry you!" In the end we felt a tremendous sense of relief that our conversation dealt in theory, not fact. We were glad we still had each other.

Trying to Make Sense of Tragedy

Why me? I have asked that question often, as many people do after suffering loss. Why did the loss happen to us? Why at such a young age? Why after trying so hard to keep the marriage together? Why in the prime of life? Why just before retirement?

Why me? Most of us want to have control of our lives. And we succeed a great deal of the time, which is due in part to the enviable powers we have at our disposal in Western civilization. We have access to good medical care, education and entertainment. We have good jobs and comfortable homes. Consequently, we have the power to get much of what we want. But the possibility of so much control makes us vulnerable to disappointment when we lose it.

Loss deprives us of control. Cancer ravages, violence erupts, divorce devastates, unemployment frustrates and death strikes—often with little warning. Suddenly we are forced to face our limitations squarely. Our expectations blow up in our face. We wonder what has gone wrong. We resent the intrusion, the inconvenience, the derailment. It is not something we were planning on! "Why me?" we ask.

I once heard someone ask the opposite question. "Why not me?" It was not a fatalistic question because he is not a fatalistic person. He asked it after his wife died of cancer. He said that suffering is simply a part of life. They had been married for 30 years, raised their children, served their community, and enjoyed many happy moments together. Then the time came to experience another side of life, the darker and more painful side.

He could no more explain why his life had turned bad than he could explain why his life had been so good up to that point. Did he choose to grow up in a stable family? Did he have control over where he was born, when he was born, or to whom he was born? Did he determine his height, weight, intelligence and appearance? Was he a better person than some baby born to a poor family in Bangladesh? He concluded that much of life seems just to happen: it is beyond our control. "Why not me?" is as good a question to ask as any.

A Global Perspective

This man has perspective. He understands his own loss in the light of global experience. The former Soviet Union lost nearly 20 million people during World War II, and that on top of the millions [Joseph] Stalin had exterminated in the 1930s. Virtually every family was touched by death. Europe lost a quarter of its population during the first phase of the Black Death [plague] from 1347–50. Hundreds of millions of people in the

Third World live under conditions of such deprivation that they rarely see prosperity, to say nothing of experiencing it. They hardly know what they are missing. Youth growing up in many inner cities witness violence and drug addiction so often that it is as common to them as green lawns and friendly neighbors are to most of us who live in the suburbs. Millions of people endure abuse of one kind or another. "Why me?" seems to be the wrong question to ask. "Why not me?" is closer to the mark, once we consider how most people live.

I realized soon after the accident that I had just been initiated into a fellowship of suffering that spans the world. My tragedy introduced me to a side of life that most people around the world know all too well. Even now I hardly qualify, considering the good life I have been privileged to live for so many years and live even today. I still have a great deal of control. I belong to a wonderful community of people. I can afford a part-time nanny. I have a secure job with flexible hours and good benefits. I have a good heritage from which to draw strength and wisdom.

The accident was really a brief, albeit dramatic, interruption in an otherwise happy, secure and prosperous life. I am still white, still male, still American, still middle-class, still employed, still established, still loved. To many people I am even heroic, which is ironic to me, since I have only done what people around the world have been doing for centuries— make the most of a bad situation. So why not me? Can I expect to live an entire lifetime free of disappointment and suffering? Free of loss and pain? The very expectation strikes me as not only unrealistic but also arrogant. God spare me from such a perfect life!

Thoughts on Fairness and Justice

Why me? Most of us want life not only to be under our control but also to be fair. So when we suffer loss, we claim our right to justice and resent circumstances that get in the way. We demand to live in a society in which virtue is rewarded and vice punished, hard work succeeds and laziness fails, decency wins and meanness loses. We feel violated when life does not turn out that way, when we get what we do not deserve and do not get what we feel we do deserve.

I do not believe for a moment that in the accident I got what I deserved. I am not perfect and never will be, but I am certainly no worse and maybe even better than some other people who seem to have it all. The explanation that people suffer or prosper according to their merits is too simple, for it does not square with human experience. I know the mother of four children, a woman not yet 40, whose husband recently died in an airplane crash. She is the epitome of goodness, kindness and honesty, as was her husband. What did she do to deserve such a loss? I know another woman, close to 80, who neglected and abused her three children while they were growing up, divorced two men because she was sick of being married to them, smokes and drinks constantly, and yet has good health, financial security and many friends. What has she done to deserve such blessing?

Eight months after the accident the alleged driver of the other car was tried in federal court on four counts of vehicular manslaughter. I was issued a subpoena to be a witness for the prosecution, which meant that once again I had to face the man whom I had met on the road shortly after the accident. I dreaded this trip to Boise [Idaho], where the trial was held. I was so nervous I actually got sick. I did not want revenge, but I did want justice so that the man whom I considered responsible for the deaths of four people—his wife and three people in my family—would pay the just penalty for his wrongdoing. At least then there would be some vindication for the suffering he had caused.

The prosecution was confident of victory. The case seemed so obvious. But the defense attorney argued that no one could actually prove that the accused had been driving the car, since both he and his wife had been thrown from the vehicle. So the burden of proof was put on the prosecution. A witness saw the accused get into the driver's seat only ten minutes before the accident occurred. Other witnesses heard the accused admit after the accident that he had been the driver of the car. But the defense attorney was able to cast enough suspicion on the testimony of these witnesses to gain an acquittal for his client.

I was enraged after the trial, which in my mind turned out to be as unjust as the accident itself. The driver did not get what he deserved any more than the victims, whether living or dead, had gotten what they deserved. The travesty of the trial became a symbol for the unfairness of the accident itself. I had to work hard to fight off cynicism.

Getting What We Deserve

Yet over time I began to be bothered by this assumption that I had a right to complete fairness. Granted, I did not deserve to lose three members of my family. But then again, I am not sure I deserved to have them in the first place. Lynda was a woman of superior qualities, and she loved me through some very hard times. My mother lived well and served people to her life's end, and she showed a rare sensitivity to me during my rebellious teenage years. Diana Jane sparkled with enthusiasm for life and helped to fill our home with noise and excitement. Perhaps I did not deserve their deaths; but I did not deserve their presence in my life either. On the face of it, living in a perfectly fair world appeals to me. But deeper reflection makes me wonder. In such a world I might never experience tragedy; but neither would I experience grace, especially the grace God gave me in the form of the three wonderful people whom I lost. . . .

I would prefer to take my chances living in a universe in which I get what I do not deserve. . . . That means that I will suffer loss, as I already have, but it also means I will receive mercy. Life will end up being far worse than it would have otherwise been; it will also end up being far better. I will have to endure the bad I do not deserve; I will also get the good I do not deserve. I dread experiencing undeserved pain, but it is worth it to me if I can also experience undeserved grace.

Desiring Grace over Fairness

If I have learned anything over the past three years, it is that I desperately need and desire the grace of God. Grace has come to me in ways I did not expect. Friends have remained loyal and supportive, in spite of my struggles. Quietness, contentment and simplicity have gradually found a place in the center of my soul, though I have never been busier. I go to bed at night grateful for the events of the day, which I try to review and reflect on until I fall asleep, and I wake up in the morning eager to begin a new day. My life is rich and productive, like Iowa farmland in late summer.

My children have become a constant source of joy to me, however demanding my role as a single parent.

Almost every day I take a few moments to listen to them practice their instruments, play a game with them, shoot a few baskets, talk about the day, and read aloud to them. When they go to bed, I always follow them down to their rooms and tuck them in. And just before I crawl into bed, I sneak into their bedrooms and pray God's blessing upon them, a practice I learned from Lynda. For four years now I have coached David's soccer team, and I occasionally take Catherine out to dinner or a concert. John, my youngest, is my constant companion; friends call him my clone and shadow.

Despite the fact that I had been a Christian for many years before the accident, since then God has become a living reality to me as never before. My confidence in God is somehow quieter but stronger. I feel little pressure to impress God or prove myself to him; yet I want to serve him with all my heart and strength. My life is full of bounty, even as I continue to feel the pain of loss. Grace is transforming me, and it is wonderful. I have slowly learned where God belongs and have allowed him to assume that place—at the center of life rather than at the periphery.

So, God spare us a life of fairness! To live in a world with grace is better by far than to live in a world of absolute fairness. A fair world might make life nice for us, but only as nice as we are. We might get what we deserve, but I wonder how much that is and whether or not we would really be satisfied. A world with grace will give us more than we deserve it, will give us life, even in our suffering.

A Son's Participation in Hindu Death Rituals for His Father

Vikas Kamat

In this piece Vikas Kamat describes how he chose to participate in traditional Hindu death rituals after his father's death. Kamat believes these rituals, which involve shaving his head, burning a grass replica of his father's body, and feeding rice balls to crows, will assist his father in his journey to heaven.

My father was a very rational man and did not believe in blind rituals. I myself do not believe in namesake rituals, and want to do my part to eliminate dark myths and idolatry from Hinduism.

Father's sudden death (he died of cardiac arrest at home) left me and my mother in deep shock. While the relatives wanted to arrange a big funeral preserving and parading the body, both my mother and I agreed that immediate disposal of father's body was both hygienic and apt for a man who lived such a simple and austere life. So there was no visitation, no cold-storing of the corpse, or other fanfare. A simple and quiet cremation was arranged. My mother went ahead and even donated my father's eyes.

Participating in the Rituals

On the ninth day (nine days symbolizing the nine months of gestation before human birth), I tonsured (shaved) my head in sacrifice and began my duty (known as *kriya*) to send father's soul to heaven. I bathed in a waterfall and performed the worship of the sun facing to the East.

Some of the raw materials used in the rituals were hay (dharba), sesame-seeds (teela), rice, and flowers.

Vikas Kamat, "How I Sent My Father to Heaven," www.kamat.com, March 18, 2002. Copyright © 1996–2006 Kamat's Potpourri. All rights reserved. Reproduced by permission.

Head shaving is one of three traditional Hindu death rituals that are thought to assist the deceased into heaven. © Christine Kolisch/Corbis.

I re-enacted the cremation by burning father's bones, a grass replica of his body, and flowers and rice symbolizing his material acquisitions. I asked [that] his spirit be liberated from all earthly bonding.

It is believed in Hinduism that the departed soul travels through the *pretaloka* (the world of ghosts and spirits) to the *pitraloka* (the heaven or the world of ancestors), and I initiated many rituals to aid the journey. The gods were invited and offerings were made.

Liberating Father's Soul

Specially prepared rice balls called *pindas* were fed to the crows, cows, and the river. The rituals continued on the tenth and eleventh day of the death.

There is a belief that unfulfilled desires of the dead prevent the soul from liberating. This is indicated by the refusal of the crow to eat the *pinda*. I invited the crow to eat the *pindas*, saying that crows were my fathers favorite birds. The crows came near the food, but did not bite. The gathered relatives asked me if I knew of any unfulfilled wishes of father. I promised publicly that I'd continue to run his website and that I'd preserve his cameras and letters. As if they understood, lots more crows approached, but none would bite yet. The crowd exclaimed that there must be something else, and I promised to my father that I'd take good care of mother. Again, as if they heard my thoughts, the crows ate away the rice balls.

My non-believing heart had melted and I once again saluted my father's dedication to my mother.

I asked that henceforth half the fruits of my charity (or divine credits) and good work be credited to my parents. On the twelfth day, I invited the spirits of the ancestors (my grand father, great grand father, and great great grand father) into new *pindas*, and asked them to receive the spirit of my father, which I had initiated into a separate rice ball. Then I broke the ball that represented father and merged it into the ancestors. This process, known as *Sapindikarana*, marked the end of father's journey.

The End of Mourning

The obliging crows reported that father indeed [had] reached the heavens! In gratitude, I honored the brahmins [honored members of the community] by giving them gifts and fed the relatives. This is known as *Samaradhana* or celebration and marked the end of mourning.

The gathered relatives sang father's laurels, read his letters, and we thanked the Lord for letting us come in contact with such a wonderful human being.

Throughout the process, I remembered one thing my mother told me "*Shraddha*, the word for last rites in Hinduism, is derived from *Shruddha*, which means religious duty or devotion. So it doesn't matter if you don't do the rituals. But whatever you do, do it with *shruddha*."

A Muslim Woman's Reflections on the Loss of Her Mother

Santi Soekanto

Santi Soekanto has worked as a journalist for seventeen years, most recently as the national desk editor at the Jakarta Post *in Indonesia. In this piece she describes the death of her mother and how her Muslim faith played an important role in providing a peaceful transition for her mother from this life to the next. Soekanto also finds peace in the midst of loss through passages in the Muslim holy book, the Koran (or Qur'an).*

Verily, to Allah belongs what He took and to Him belongs what He gave and everything with Him has an appointed time.

My mother, Surtiningsih Wiryo Taruno, died beautifully in my arms Tuesday morning, May 3, 2005, after a very long fight with an illness that had forced her to struggle for breath. My father and my sisters were present at her last moments, reciting the Qur'an to usher her into the Hereafter. I witnessed how she drew her last breath as gently as the sudden rain that fell outside the windows of the clinic where she had been treated for the past two weeks.

Pain had been my mother's constant companion for years, more so after she was diagnosed in 2001 with breast cancer, which later spread to lungs already ravaged by TB [tuberculosis] and other infections. She also struggled with heart and hyperthyroid problems. But she had never been idle or unproductive in her life.

Santi Soekanto, "Of Faith and Death: A Muslim Woman's Reflections on Loss," www .islamonline.net, May 18, 2005. Reproduced by permission of the author.

A Mother's Legacy

She gave birth to nine children and raised seven of us to adulthood, always telling us that she would not care if our school reports were full of bad marks, but that she would never, ever tolerate wickedness and meanness in her children. She brought us up to be decent people, and she raised all her five daughters to be accomplished women and fighters. "It doesn't matter if you have a flat nose or if you limp, but you girls have to grow up strong," she always told us.

She wrote dozens of children's books, several of them jointly with my father, Soekanto S. A., who wrote more than 30 children's books. In the early 1980s when [Indonesian] President Soeharto's intelligence agents spied on any Islamic movements or activities, she risked her own and our safety for *da 'wah* [inviting others to Islam] by opening up her house for Qur'anic studies. She would stand outside on the lookout, in case any suspicious people passed by and noticed the gathering. She designed and had Muslim dresses made for girls so they could appear nice while adhering to the Islamic ruling on how a Muslim woman should dress.

She was instrumental in helping build the foundation for what is known today as the Tarbiyah Islamic Movement, because she basically supported the forming of the earliest cadres of that movement. She read the Qur'an haltingly because when she was a little girl growing up in a small city in East Java [Indonesia], she was not taught well, but she memorized a great deal of the translation of the Qur'an by H. B. Jassin.

Finding Comfort in Words of Faith

She was a devout Muslim, and this remained evident in her last days that were filled with pain and an incessant, racking cough. By her last day, she was struggling to breathe, even with the help of continuous oxygen, but she still said her prayers and she put her affairs in order. From her bed, she told one of my sisters to prepare food "for the guests who are coming." She waved her hand toward the door and told us to open it because "the guests are coming." She told us that she looked toward us with blessings.

In her last hour, she slid from her bed to the floor, still unable to breathe properly, but no longer struggling. She said she was tired. I stopped praying for her recovery and began to pray for a good ending, a gentle death. She slept briefly on my sister's chest then she woke up and asked whether she had died. My sister said, "No of course you're not dead, here, feel my kisses."

At around 1 a.m., all the fight went out of her and I could see the change in her pallor. She became so white, her breathing became labored. We recited the Qur'an. My father sat in front of her, declaring how pleased he was with her, that she had his blessings, despite the fact that she was a much better wife than he ever deserved.

A gentle rain fell outside of the window. I gathered my weakened, fighter mother into my arms, and I whispered into her ears, "Astaghfiru Allah Al-'Azhim, la ilaha illa Allah, Muhammad Rasul Allah. Please God forgive me. We testify that there is no God but Allah and that Muhammad is the Messenger of Allah." This was the prayer that the Prophet Muhammad taught Muslims to recite to somebody on their deathbed.

A Peaceful Death

Her breathing became even slower, and a long sigh escaped her open lips. That was her last breath. I placed my right hand on her heart and felt no beating. I touched her wrist and found no pulse. The doctor came in to confirm what I knew already, that my mother had passed on.

The rain stopped and peace descended upon my beautiful, beautiful, Muslimah mujahidah [Muslim fighter]. I placed my lips on her forehead, now no longer marred by the frowns that resulted from having to endure so much pain, and whispered, "Raditu billahi Rabba, wa bil-Islami deena, wa bi Muhammadin nabiya wa rasula. I accept and am pleased that Allah is my God, that Islam is my religion, and that Muhammad is my Prophet and Messenger."

Her five daughters and two daughters-in-law bathed her after the Fajr Prayer and we said prayers to send her off, flying through the seven skies in the protective hands of the angels. We laid her to rest and told her we would continue with the jihad [struggle] to be good Muslims.

Beloved mom, till we meet again.

SOCIAL ISSUES
FIRSTHAND

Choosing the Moment of Death

Why I Chose to End My Life

Carol Bernstein Ferry

Carol Bernstein Ferry grew up in Portland, Maine, and worked for a time as a copyeditor and proofreader for various publishers in New York. Ferry was an outspoken financial supporter of various leftist causes, opposing the Vietnam War and supporting prisoners' rights and nuclear disarmament.

The following selection is a letter Ferry wrote to explain her reasons for deciding to take an overdose of sleeping pills to end her life after being diagnosed with terminal illness at the age of seventy-six. She rallies her family to support her decision to end her life. She remarks on the long and happy life she has had and her desire to end her life without pain and suffering. She states that she would prefer to have a loved one help her with the administration of the lethal substance in order to ensure that she was successful in her attempt. She laments, however, that since assisted suicide is illegal, she must commit the act on her own.

If my death can contribute to an understanding of euthanasia, then I want it to do so. That is why I am writing this letter, explaining why I choose to take active steps to end my life rather than waiting for death to come gradually. With this letter I also want to make it clear that, although I have the support and tacit agreement of my children and close friends, no one but myself will take the steps that cause death. It is unfortunate that I must say this; our laws are at a destructive point just now, so if anyone other than myself actually causes my death, that person will be liable to conviction as a felon. What an absurdity! To help someone facing a time—whether short or long—of pain and distress, whose death coming bit by bit can cause major sorrow and anxiety to family and

Carol Bernstein Ferry, "A Good Death," *Nation*, vol. 273, September 17, 2001, p. 8.

friends, not to mention the medical help, quite useless, that must be expended in order to maintain a bearable level of pain—that this sensible deed can be construed a crime is a blot on our legal system and on our power of thought.

I have known since last June [2000] that I am terminally ill. Emphysema, a tumor in my chest and recently a new tumor near my pelvis put it beyond question that I am on the way to death. This seems to me in no way a tragedy—I am, after all, 76 years old—but a natural ending. I don't feel called upon to suffer until the last minute of a creeping death, nor do I want to put my children through such a time, so I am choosing to make a finish while I am still able to function.

Reflecting on Life and a Peaceful End

I've had a lucky life. I've had a lot of joy; I've had enough sorrow to know that I'm a member in good standing of the human race; I have tried to make myself useful. I have nothing to complain about, certainly not death. I feel lucky now, in that I have been given a somewhat definite span of life ahead. Once the approximate limit of that span—six months to a year from last June—got absorbed into my brain, many problems floated away. I no longer have to worry about death, as it is with me now. Every day is a treat, an extra gift, the positive side of the expression Borrowed Time. It is my hope that people close to me, especially my children, can also enjoy this relaxed attitude toward something that is, after all, inevitable. The idea that I can probably manage to have a peaceful and relatively painless ending is a comfort. For that probability to be a certainty would be the best comfort of all. But that certainty could only come if I were to have the help of a second person, and that I will not have, as under present law that person would be in immediate danger.

Considering the Moral Arguments

The moral beauty of suffering for its own sake is important to many, for reasons that I find unfathomable. Religious pres-

Although suicide is illegal in most states, many people ignore suicide laws in order to choose their moment of death. © Angelo Cavalli/zefa/Corbis.

sure, the idea that God enjoys our suffering, is beyond me. And the terrible attitude of our lawmakers and politicians, considering that any help toward a painless death should be punished, is a source of wonder and shame. A few states—notably Oregon and Maine—are trying to change their laws to allow the administration of painkilling medicine even if it hastens the moment of death. Even this moderate and humane act is being fought in legislatures of some states and in the Senate. The idea that human life is sacred no matter the condition or the desire of the person seems to me irrational.

The people who think that it is immoral to make a rational decision about ending life certainly have the right to consider their own death in this light and to endure to the very end whatever pain awaits them and their families. But they have flowed over into the idea that it is their right also to control those others of us who view the matter differently. There are societies here and there that do not put up roadblocks when a person decides to end life. However, the idea that each person's life is his own is too radical or too abstruse for consumption in the United States. This is the attitude that I hope will change, and soon. It is the attitude that I hope to help soften by explaining that my suicide plan is bringing me and those close to me a measure of security that my life can end in as spirited a way as possible.

A Thoughtful Decision

I appreciate everyone who has been involved in encouraging me, including those who have not encouraged me but who have withstood the temptation to reprimand me. My decision has been arrived at after many years of contemplation, not quickly or casually. I hope it will help others to feel all right about preferring a peaceful, benign path into death.

Coping with a Friend's Suicide

Patricia Volk

Patricia Volk is an author who has written novels, short stories, and articles for various well-known magazines. She was a weekly columnist for New York Newsday. *The following piece describes the difficult journey Volk was left to experience after the suicide of her best friend twenty-three years earlier. Volk struggled with guilt for many years because she knew her friend was suicidal but did not tell her friend's parents. She wonders if there was something more she could have said or done to prevent the death. After years of regret and wanting more answers, she comes to understand that she will never know more about why her friend chose suicide. She ultimately accepts that there was nothing she could have done to prevent the death.*

Twenty-three years ago, she took her own life. But looking back isn't about pain anymore. It's about honoring the fact that this fine woman lived.

"There's a packet of letters tied with a ribbon in the bottom drawer of my dresser," I tell my son on the phone, "under the quilted glove box."

I am in San Francisco, the city where my best friend killed herself 23 years ago. It's been almost a quarter of a century since then, but suddenly I want her old address. I want to see where it happened.

We met when we were 12, the year my family moved from New York City to the suburbs. We liked each other right away. Both of us annoyed people by always asking "Why?" We asked each other "Why?" a lot too. Our favorite sentence was: "What does it mean?" We were going to be painters.

When Something Truly Terrible happens, the way you feel about it changes. It changes because you and the world around

Patricia Volk, "Remembering My Best Friend," *Good Housekeeping*, July 2000, p. 92.

74

you change. Your feelings about it keep changing too. You go through phases. I didn't know that when my friend died.

Getting the News

The call came at 5:30 on a Sunday morning. I was married and living in New York City, seven months into my first pregnancy.

"How?" I sobbed into the phone.

"Pills," her half sister said from San Francisco. "There was a letter to you in the typewriter."

"Did you read it?"

"Yes."

"Can I have it?"

"No."

I called my friend's parents. If grief had weight, that conversation would have sunk us. Before we said good-bye, they asked me to tell anyone who asked that their daughter had died in a car accident. Whatever they wanted, anything, even if I had to lie.

After I hung up, my husband held me while I cried. I thought about a night when my friend and I were 13. Lost in one of our endless conversations, she had burned holes in my bedspread with the ash from her cigarette.

We'd never talk together in the dark again. We'd never talk about what things meant. I'd never see my friend again. She was gone.

From seventh grade through twelfth, we lived two streets apart. During junior high, we rode our bikes to secret places—a haunted house, a beach paved with hermit crabs. We experimented with beauty rituals using styling gel and sliced cucumbers. On Saturdays, we'd head for a photo booth at Woolworth, posing and wondering why we hadn't been discovered by a Hollywood talent scout. When she was 27, her parents retired to Los Angeles, and she decided to give San Francisco a try.

Dealing with the Guilt

Grief is a journey. As I grappled with it, my initial sense of loss gave way to a new phase: guilt. What if I hadn't listened to my friend? What if I'd betrayed her confidence and told her family that she was talking about suicide? Would she still be alive? What if I'd gone out to California to see her when she'd wanted me to?

We'd spoken on the phone every night for three months before she died. I knew she was depressed.

"I'm going to kill myself," she had been saying in a dark, jokey way.

"Why?" I asked.

"Why not?"

I attributed her depression to a busted romance. I could always make my friend laugh and, I reasoned, people who laugh don't kill themselves, right?

"How are you going to do it?" I asked. Then she told me, and I told her why it wouldn't work. Jump from the Golden Gate Bridge? You'll mash your nose job. Gas? It can leave you even stupider. Guns? Suppose you live?

"What do your parents say?" I asked.

"I'm not telling them."

"Then I will."

"If you do, I'll never speak to you again. I mean it."

She was blowtorching relationships, furious at everyone. I thought I could be more helpful if I wasn't exiled. So we talked and talked—as if talking about suicide could substitute for the act.

"Come to me," she said.

"No, I'm pregnant," I replied. "You come to me."

Then her doctor admitted her to the hospital.

"But there's really nothing wrong with me," she explained over the phone. "I have hypoglycemia and thyroiditis. Mental wards are filled with people who really have hypoglycemia and thyroiditis."

One night a friend of hers called to tell me he was worried. Then I got scared. I called my friend's doctor. He said she was depressed and "difficult." Against advice, she had signed herself out of the hospital.

"Come to me," she said when she called.

"I can't. You come to me." Twenty-three years later, on my second day in San Francisco, I phone my son again. "Try looking in my sewing table. Maybe her letters are there. Her envelopes were airmail."

He can't find the old correspondence, and I can't remember the name of my friend's street. Lombard? Filbert? Clay? I walk around the city and wonder: What will I do if I find the building? Ring the bell and ask the super if he knew her? Why do I need to see where she lived and died?

Dealing with the Blame

When you learn about an unexpected death, it takes time for your brain to catch up with the news. After the call about my friend, I kept thinking I saw her on the bus or walking toward me. She had a look. She'd bleached her hair to emulate Carol Lynley, a hot model of our youth. And she'd invented a way of walking, placing one foot directly in front of the other. She owned that walk. To her, it radiated grace.

I honored her parents' request about how she died. Only my husband and parents knew the truth.

Three years after my friend's suicide, I had another baby. A month later, I flew to Los Angeles on business. My friend's mother did not want to see me, but her father agreed to meet me in a restaurant.

"We've stopped blaming you," he said over salad.

"You blamed me?"

"You knew she was unhappy, and you didn't call us."

"She told me I couldn't."

From the moment I realized my friend's family blamed me, I stopped blaming myself. Guilt peeled off me like a rubber glove. This is when I entered the next phase of my grief: resignation. My new way of looking at my friend's suicide was: No one can stop anyone who really wants to do it.

The day after I had lunch with my friend's father, her mother called and said she had decided to talk to me.

I remembered her as a woman who made Jell-o molds, wore her hair in a pixie, and served her guests on sleek teak trays. She'd drifted around the house in stenciled eyebrows with a drink in her hand and a cigarette bobbing between her lips. I thought she was wildly sophisticated.

"May I see the letter that was in the typewriter?" I asked. "It would mean so much to me."

"No."

All I wanted was to see that letter, to know my friend's last words to me. Was she loving? Angry? Did her family not want me to see the letter because she had blamed them? Were they protecting me because she'd blamed me?

The Letters

After my visit to Los Angeles, my friend's father and I corresponded for a while. He wasn't feeling well. Then he went on dialysis. Then he stopped writing. Two years ago, I wrote to my friend's mother at the old address. The letter came back RETURN TO SENDER. I tried to locate a new address, but there was no listing. I thought, I've kept their secret till now. My friend's been dead longer than I knew her.

Here's what I miss most: our easy, risk-free intimacy, having her know and love my kids, and seeing her married with her own children to love.

When someone you love dies, your shared past goes with them. Part of me is missing now.

When I get home from San Francisco, I find the letters. She lived on Fillmore. I was on Fillmore. From her first letter after leaving New York for San Francisco: The phone just rang, a new friend. I'm meeting people more easily, liking them better, accepting them more, all, obviously, because I like and accept myself more than in years. It's as though I've just recovered from a prolonged nervous breakdown ... I feel well and whole again ... I'm really happy to be here. Something or someone very good is going to happen. I feel it strongly.

And from the last one she mailed, two years later: This started out as a love letter and turned to confession and self-pity. Bear with me: I stopped my medication completely and now find myself totally exhausted by a burst of nervous energy, which doesn't stop to let me sleep at night. And no matter how tired my body gets, I can't shut off my mind.

And on (gratefully) to happier things.

Regret and Acceptance

How valid is memory? Not very. The truth about my friend's suicide keeps changing. With this writing, another phase has begun. I'm getting used to not knowing what I would like to know. I can't know if flying out there would have made a difference. I can't know if telling her family or consulting an expert would have either, though, God, I wish I had. And I can't know what was in the letter. I fantasize that my friend's half sister, whom I rarely saw but liked, will read this and find a way to contact me. I would love to talk to someone who loved my friend. I would love the chance to express the regret I feel because I wasn't smart enough to help.

Meanwhile, accepting that I can't have answers has begun to feel like an achievement. Resolved: I will never have resolution about my friend's suicide, I'll never know if things could have been different. Closure is not possible. So I'll just take her suicide through life with me, turning it over the way a squirrel turns a nut. As I change, it will change. And in that odd way, my friend and I will grow old together. Remembering her isn't about pain anymore. It's about honoring the fact that she lived, and my luck in having had such a fine friend.

Weeks go by when I don't think of her. But never years. Loss is like an old car: It fades; you get used to it. Which is not to say it ever goes away.

Near-Death
Experiences and
the Afterlife

A Near-Death Experience Brings a Woman to Faith in God

Beverly Brodsky

Beverly Brodsky was raised in a conservative Jewish home. When she learned in school about the killing of millions of Jewish people during World War II, however, she decided that there was no God. In her early twenties Brodsky had a serious motorcycle accident that led to a near-death experience that had an intensely emotional impact on her. In the following selection she provides a vivid and detailed description of what happened to her during that time. Brodsky is surprised that even she finds herself in the presence of God after death, and she experiences great joy, love, and peace. She also asks God the many difficult questions she has about the Holocaust of the Jewish people and finds all knowledge and truth. From her experience, Brodsky claims to have learned that death does not exist and love does not end.

Somehow an unexpected peace descended upon me. I found myself floating on the ceiling over the bed looking down at my unconscious body. I barely had time to realize the glorious strangeness of the situation—that I was me but not in my body—when I was joined by a radiant being bathed in a shimmering white glow. Like myself, this being flew but had no wings. I felt a reverent awe when I turned to him; this was no ordinary angel or spirit, but he had been sent to deliver me. Such love and gentleness emanated from his being that I felt that I was in the presence of the messiah.

Whoever he was, his presence deepened my serenity and awakened a feeling of joy as I recognized my companion.

Beverly Brodsky, as quoted in Kenneth Ring's *Lessons from the Light: What We Can Learn from the Near-Death Experience.* New York: Insight Books, Plenum Press, 1998. Copyright © 1998 Kenneth Ring. Reprinted by permission of Da Capo Press, a member of Perseus Books, L.L.C.

Gently he took my hand and we flew right through the window. I felt no surprise at my ability to do this. In this wondrous presence, everything was as it should be. . . .

Beneath us lay the beautiful Pacific Ocean, over which I had excitedly watched the sun set when I had first arrived [in Los Angeles]. But my attention was now directed upward, where there was a large opening leading to a circular path. Although it seemed to be deep and far to the end, a white light shone through and poured out into the gloom to the other side where the opening beckoned. It was the most brilliant light I had ever seen, although I didn't realize how much of its glory was veiled from the outside. The path was angled upward, obliquely, to the right. Now, still hand in hand with the angel, I was led into the opening of the small, dark passageway.

In the Presence of the All-Knowing God

I then remember traveling a long distance upward toward the light. I believe that I was moving very fast, but this entire realm seemed to be outside of time. Finally, I reached my destination. It was only when I emerged from the other end that I realized that I was no longer accompanied by the being who had brought me there. But I wasn't alone. There, before me, was the living presence of the Light. Within it I sensed an all-pervading intelligence, wisdom, compassion, love, and truth. There was neither form nor sex to this perfect Being. It, which I shall in the future call He, in keeping with our commonly accepted syntax, contained everything, as white light contains all the colors of a rainbow when penetrating a prism. And deep within me came an instant and wondrous recognition: I, even I, was facing God.

I immediately lashed out at Him with all the questions I had ever wondered about; all the injustices I had seen in the physical world. I don't know if I did this deliberately, but I discovered that God knows all your thoughts immediately and responds telepathically. My mind was naked; in fact, I became pure mind. The ethereal body which I had traveled in through the tunnel seemed to be no more; it was just my personal intelligence confronting that Universal Mind, which clothed itself in a glorious, living light that was more felt than seen, since no eye could absorb its splendor.

I don't recall the exact content of our discussion; in the process of return, the insights that came so clearly and fully in Heaven were not brought back with me to Earth. I'm sure that I asked the question that had been plaguing me since childhood about the sufferings of my people. I do remember this: There was a reason for *everything* that happened, no matter how awful it appeared in the physical realm. And within myself, as I was given the answer, my own awakening mind now responded in the same manner: "Of course," I would think, "I already know that. How could I ever have forgotten!" Indeed, it appears that all that happens is for a purpose, and that purpose is already known to our eternal self.

In time the questions ceased, because I suddenly was filled with all the Being's wisdom. I was given more than just the answers to my questions; all knowledge unfolded to me, like the instant blossoming of an infinite number of flowers all at once. I was filled with God's knowledge, and in that precious aspect of his Beingness, I was one with him. But my journey of discovery was just beginning.

A Journey with the God of Love

Now I was treated to an extraordinary voyage through the universe. Instantly we traveled to the center of stars being born, supernovas exploding, and many other glorious celestial events for which I have no name. The impression I have now of this trip is that it felt like the universe is all one grand object woven from the same fabric. Space and time are illusions that hold us to our plane; out there all is present simultaneously. I was a passenger on a Divine spaceship in which the Creator showed me the fullness and beauty of all of his Creation.

The last thing that I saw before all external vision ended was a glorious fire—the core and center of a marvelous star. Perhaps this was a symbol for the blessing that was now to come to me. Everything faded except for a richly full void in which That and I encompassed All that is. Here, I experienced, in ineffable magnificence, communion with the Light Being. Now I was filled with not just all knowledge, but also with all love. It was as if the Light were poured in and through me. I was God's object of adoration; and from His/our love I drew life and joy beyond imagining. My being was transformed; my delusions, sins, and guilt were forgiven and purged without asking; and now I was Love, primal Being, and bliss. And, in some sense, I remain there, for Eternity. Such a union cannot be broken. It always was, is, and shall be.

Suddenly, not knowing how or why, I returned to my broken body. But miraculously, I brought back the love and the joy. I was filled with an ecstasy beyond my wildest dreams. Here, in my body, the pain had all been removed. I was still enthralled by a boundless delight. For the next two months, I remained in this state, oblivious to any pain . . .

I felt now as if I had been made anew. I saw wondrous meanings everywhere; everything was alive and full of energy and intelligence. . . .

Although it's been twenty years since my heavenly voyage, I have never forgotten it. Nor have I, in the face of ridicule and disbelief, ever doubted its reality. Nothing that intense and life-changing could possibly have been a dream or hallucination. To the contrary, I consider the rest of my life to be a passing fantasy, a brief dream, that will end when I again awaken in the permanent presence of that giver of life and bliss.

For those who grieve or fear, I assure you of this: There is no death, nor does love ever end. And remember also that we are aspects of the one perfect whole, and as such are part of God, and of each other. Someday you who are reading this and I will be together in light, love, and unending bliss.

A Woman Chooses to Live to Raise Her Son

Karen Schaeffer

Karen Schaeffer is a mother and teacher who was involved in a car accident seven months after the birth of her first child, a son. At that time she experienced a near-death event that she describes in the following piece. Schaeffer describes the place that she went to as peaceful, beautiful, and serene. Yet, she was not able to forget her son and her desire to raise him. She was shown that in the future her husband would eventually remarry. Her son would be cared for, but not in the way a biological mother cares for her child. This caused her such distress that she was allowed to return to her life and raise her son. Still, she remembers the love and joy she experienced in the afterlife and longs to experience it again.

As a teenager, I had several psychic experiences, often occurring in dreams. As I grew older and life more hectic, these experiences diminished—almost disappeared until the pregnancy of my first child.

Shortly after his birth I had the most horrific dream that I would be in a terrible car crash that would take my life. For months I was terrified and was extremely cautious and on the lookout for that monster vehicle. By the time my son was 7 months old, I convinced myself it was only a dream . . . nothing of what was to come. I had a brand new teaching position, a baby, a home and my husband to take care of . . . I had put too much energy into this thing. Then it happened.

I had left school right away that day. I wanted to pick up my son from his grandmother and hurry back to school to watch a baseball game. It was a picture perfect way to spend the afternoon with my son. As I was exiting the freeway with usual caution, I made a left hand turn on a light that had been green for some time. This was my lucky day I thought. Then in an instant I was gone.

Experiencing the Afterlife

Immediately I was in the most beautiful, serene place I had ever been. My grandfather, another person whom I had known in a previous life, and a guardian were ready to help me with the transition. They told me of the accident, showed me the site. It was my time to come home they said.

The overwhelming love and happiness of that place was so inviting.

I could feel myself becoming lighter each moment. In a fit of fear and panic I began crying. No, I couldn't be dead. What would happen to my son? He was seven months old! He would never remember me. His father didn't even know how to take care of him. I didn't want him raised by his father's parents. No, no, no . . . this was not the time to go. They were wrong.

In an embrace of love they calmed me by showing me that my son, my entire family would be okay after my death. My mother could lean on my grandmother. It would take time, but she would heal. My husband, hurt, sad, and lonely would also heal and eventually find love once again.

Death is part of the lessons we are to learn on earth, and my death was an important lesson for those involved in my life. I was shown my funeral, taught how to be near those I loved and told I could eventually communicate with those whose spirits were open. I could accept this. They would be fine.

Unable to Let Go

I was feeling lighter all the time. But wait . . . my son. I couldn't leave my son! Babies need their mommies. I needed to be his mommy. I couldn't let go. So much patience was shown to me—so much love.

My guides explained that the feelings I was having were still a connection to my human side. Once my Humanness wore off, I would feel light as air, utter happiness, and extreme love.

Words do not do the feelings justice. They worked to help me throw off my human weight. The feelings were so great and seemed to pull me in stronger and stronger; yet my connection to my son was so strong.

We wandered in this beautiful place for what seemed an eternity. We discussed my life. We discussed religion. We discussed secrets of the soul that as humans we must forget, lest we'd never be able to thrive on earth. All the while I was in awe. Some things were just as I always dreamed an afterlife would be. Some things I was just plain wrong [about,] and I remember thinking, "Wow!" Where were my other loved ones? When could I see my other grandparents who had passed? In time—they were on a different plane. When my transition was complete I could choose to go to other levels when I was ready.

Visions of the Future and Past

Every now and then thoughts of my son would make me heavy once again. I couldn't bear the thought of him growing up without a mother. I was told others would be a mother for me. First grandparents, and then they showed me Jake's life. He was the most beautiful boy, so happy, but with a touch of sadness that seemed to pierce his soul. This was his lesson to tackle. He knew coming into this life the main lessons he was to learn. It was meant to be. I saw a new mom for Jake when he was about 7 or 8. A beautiful woman, kind-hearted, who definitely cared for Jake and treated him well, but she was to have her own child with my widowed husband and the love she showed for her own child was different and unequal to the love she showed for my child—her stepchild. This isn't what I dreamed for Jake. This couldn't be. I was happy for my husband. He was okay. He was happy. My son was a different story. Other lessons were learned in the constant-patient job of transitioning me to the other side. I had to let go. At times I became hysterical and then moments later I was calm and serene.

I saw a girl child who had been meant in Jake's place, but before conception, plans changed and there was a need for Jake's spirit to take her place. There was much upheaval that Jake could help mend (and he did).

Allowed to Return

At a time when I felt the closest to accepting my death, I experienced a resurgence of sorrow and pain, longing for my son, for my life. I couldn't let go of my human life. My guides tried their hardest. They never gave up. They never became discouraged. It is unbelievable the amount of patience and love they exuded. Finally, my hysteria was calmed by a higher spirit who seemed to envelop me in love. My guides were instructed to allow me to return. Despite their pleas to allow them more time, they were told that at this point, my spirit would not rest. It was best to let me return, to settle my spirit, learn further lessons. My pleading won my return for the time being. I understood that before my descent, my friends and family had lessons being postponed, but they would have to learn the lessons resulting from my death at some time later.

Arrangements were made for when, where, how my spirit would return and which lessons I was to have enriched or acquire new. Some lessons learned in my arrival on the other side would have to be forgotten, and it was not good for my soul to know when I was dying again or else as a human I would focus on only that, especially as the time neared.

The last things I remember were being taken back to the accident site, and just before my descent, I was told when my children were older it would be time to come home for good.

I accepted it immediately, but then, wait! What qualifies as older? Does it mean only a few years older? Teenagers? Will I live to see them marry and have their own children? This was a difficult aspect to deal with immediately after the accident.

I had a life with my son again. I had to spend it right, for I had no idea how much longer I had left.

The Aftermath of a Near-Death Experience

I was told I was lucky to survive. A large utility truck ran a red light and hit the driver's side of my tiny compact car. Despite wearing a seatbelt the doctors say I would not have survived if it were not for the airbags [opening], something that is not supposed to happen in a side impact.

The first year after the accident was an attempt to live the best I could, the happiest I could. I was suffering, however, from severe pain from a fractured shoulder bone, broken ribs, and two hip fractures. I was told the pain should disappear in six months to a year at the worst. Three years later, the pain has not gone away. The second year, however, seemed to be the worst. I became so suicidal. All I wanted to do was to return to this place, this life so awesome, so love-filled, and so joyous. My son, and later my daughter, were the only things that made me go on. I was here for them. Today, only three years later, I have accepted my return to earth, long to return to my after-life home, and struggle to find peace and happiness until my time here comes to its final end.

A Child's Near-Death Experience and Its Impact on the Family

Doug Mendenhall

Doug Mendenhall is the author of several books describing the changes in his daughter after her near-death experience. The story began with Denise Mendenhall becoming sick and falling into a diabetic coma. The prognosis was grim, but she recovered. After the illness she was able to see people's auras, interact with Jesus, interact with dead people, and go back and live events in history. The family found themselves in an awkward position trying to explain what had happened to their daughter. At first they avoided telling others, but they came to realize that their daughter had been given a gift that they wanted to tell others about.

In the summer of 1999 our little ten-year-old daughter, Denise, was literally counting the weeks, days, hours, minutes, and seconds until school started. Denise was always a happy, sweet little girl. Soon after school started her personality changed. She was unhappy all the time claiming how much she hated school, her friends, everything. Then she started going to the bathroom all the time and drinking tons of water. She would get sick and just not feel well. We asked several medical people that lived in the neighborhood about the symptoms she was displaying, and were told it was probably just a virus. One even was a diabetic nurse and another one was a medical doctor! It was like they were shielded from seeing that it was diabetes. Her personality change was so dramatic, that we talked about getting her to see some mental health professionals.

Doug Mendenhall, "Denise—Lessons from the Spirit," www.cinemind.com/atwater, March 27, 2006. Reproduced by permission of the author.

It progressed to the point where she felt real sick on Friday, November 5 [1999]. She played in the morning with her mother, ate lunch, and asked if she could lie down for a nap. My wife went in to check on her an hour or so later and she was asleep. Then after another hour she checked on Denise again and found she hadn't moved and was breathing really strangely. She called me in and we found that her eyes had rolled back in their sockets and she was unresponsive. I called a doctor friend and he said to get her to the hospital immediately, also he would call ahead and have them ready for her. So we took off to the hospital. I literally drove over one hundred miles per hour and hit every light green.

At the hospital they descended on her. As they pulled her clothes off, I was shocked at what a skinny little girl she was. She had always been skinny, but now she looked like a little child from a third world country, skin and bones. I stared in disbelief.

They put an IV in her immediately and started checking. They told us it looked like she was in a coma and wanted to do many more tests. We sat and waited as they wheeled her off to do a CAT scan.

Near Death in a Diabetic Coma

Two hours later a neurologist took us to a room and told Dianne and me that Denise was in a coma, from the diabetes she has. But the most devastating thing was that she had suffered a stroke. It was at the base of the left side of her brain, the main artery. He then said that the left side of her brain, more than two-thirds of it, was destroyed by the stroke. The blood vessels and capillaries had fragmented like tissue paper and the blood had flowed freely. Normally they would put in a shunt and drain off the blood, but she was so far gone, they saw no reason to do so. All of her organs were shutting down. She would not live past the next twenty-four hours we were told. If by some miracle she did live, she would be a vegetable the rest of her life, never to walk or talk again.

They had put a tube down her throat to breathe for her if she quit breathing. Later we would learn that they had wanted to harvest her organs for donation, but had never brought out the forms. A 'bolt' was put into her brain to monitor the pressure, as the liquids they had to give her would make the brain swell, cutting off the circulation at the base and that also would kill her. It seems like there was no way she could live.

She stayed in the coma for three days and never quit breathing. After two days they took the tube out of her throat. At the end of the third she woke up, looked at Dianne and me and said she was hungry. The nurse looked up, startled, asking if she had just talked. I said she had, and they descended on her as she went back to sleep.

A Miraculous Recovery

The next day she woke up and stayed awake. They moved her from ICU [intensive care unit] to the third floor where we could learn to give her insulin shots. I remember that she really was a vegetable when she woke up. She was taught to do everything all over again, from talking, reading, writing, even going to the bathroom. Within three days she had progressed to the point where she walked one thousand feet that day. She truly was a miracle! The doctors really didn't know what to make of her. They would come into her room, look at her, shake their heads, and walk out. We left the hospital on November 30, 1999, twenty-five days after going in.

We figured that life would go on as normal except that we did have a miracle child with us. Though we now had to give her two injections of insulin each day for her diabetes.

One day I was trying to give her a shot of insulin and she kept fighting me. She wouldn't let me give her the shot. After forty-five minutes I was upset with her, and let her know it. She yelled, pointing her finger above my head that I 'was mad and I was red.' I asked what in the world she was talking about. 'You're mad, you're red,' she said again. I had read enough that I knew about the energy field around our body, called the aura.

"You can see auras?" I asked.

"What's that?" she responded.

I told her it was the energy around our body. She said that she could see them, since she woke up from her coma. This was the start of our family entering a world we did not know existed.

Discovering Denise's Special Gifts

Over the next month, Denise displayed many gifts or abilities and told us many things. She not only could see the aura of a person, she knew what the color meant. At this point she only saw the first level of the aura. She is able to see "spirits" as we call them, or people that have passed on (died). She sees Christ and her Heavenly Father. She can tell what kind of person you are; she sees into your heart.

The most fascinating thing she told us was that while she was in the coma for three days, she had spent that time with Jesus. She told me about his birth, life, his suffering in the garden, the cross. It was in detail, all the colors, smells, and sounds. She told me things that I knew a little ten-year-old could not know.

All of this changed our lives significantly. My wife and I have six living children, five were at home during this time. The events polarized our family somewhat. I knew in my heart Denise was telling me the truth of what she had experienced. Yet it was hard for others to understand and accept. We learned many "lessons" from our little ten-year-old daughter.

Lessons from the Afterlife

She taught us not to judge: anyone or anything. We learned of God's unconditional love for all of us. One of the biggest lessons was to be grateful for all things. Gratitude is a huge lesson we were to learn over and over. We learned that after a person dies, he or she can move on to God, or some become "earthbound." Such was the individual (spirit) that was in our home at the time. She even encountered some who would not believe they were dead! We learned that evil is real. There are dark spirits who do work for Satan or the Devil. She sees them also.

We learned through our experiences with her that we all have a guardian spirit(s) or angel(s). We had several experiences where our lives were saved by them and she saw what they did to save us. She thought it was "cool."

I guess the main spiritual impact on our lives was the fact that she spent three days with Jesus and still sees him and interacts with him on a daily basis. This has had the biggest impact on our family. One person asked Denise who her best friend is and she said, "Jesus." We ended up going out and talking to people one-on-one for the next year. All during that year she kept telling me, "Dad, you are supposed to write a book about all of this." I told her that I didn't write books and that I didn't want anyone to know about all of this. I felt that it was just too weird for most people to accept, and didn't want to invite persecution into our lives.

Going Public About Denise's Gifts

Finally at the end of the year 2000, I agreed to do a book about it. We had a friend help us write it. It was published some seven months later. We then went around and did "book reviews" where we gave them away. The book is called, *My Peace I Give Unto You*, and we gave away over seven thousand copies over the next eighteen months. From the e-mails we get it has changed many lives and helped many people find their Savior, Jesus Christ.

In May of 2002, we were prompted to write a second book. You see our experiences with Denise never quit. We are continually being taught things and are having experiences. So we published the second book in November of 2002. We have since printed over one thousand copies of it. It is called *Possibilities . . . Lessons from the Spirit.* Since we have been asked to travel all over the country telling our story, we now sell both books. That defrays our expenses somewhat, since we do not charge when we do book reviews. The books are available on a Web site at: www.publishinghope.com. At one time we had them available in some bookstores, but now we sell them at book reviews or ship them from our home or people can order from the Web site.

Living with New Abilities

Doing the book reviews has changed our lives. We have met many people with similar gifts as Denise. We have met many children and adults who see the spirits of dead people. There are dozens we've met who see auras. Others 'fly' at night when they sleep as Denise does. These people have told us our books have helped them to realize that they are not freaks, that there are many others out there similar to them, with gifts. There are others who can see into you and determine where an illness is. They have come to understand that these gifts come from a loving God and are to be used for his work. Whether they are to be used or not is the will of God, and not that of Denise or those with similar gifts. Today, our family has learned to live with a daughter/sister who lives in both worlds, the one the rest of us see and the other one that few others see. She enjoys meeting people that have lived before. When she sleeps she can go back in the past and see events. She has witnessed all of the Bible. She fell in love with the movie *Titanic* when it aired on television and went back to see what it was really like. At first, being able to do this made it difficult for her to attend our church. When people put their own interpretation on biblical events she would turn to me and say, "Dad that's not how it really happened." Now she goes to enjoy the people and be around kids her own age.

She prefers to be a normal kid, yet knows that she is not. She likes to be around friends who "know about" her, yet treat her as any other friend. Being a fourteen-year-old, she loves to talk about the cutest boys, etc. Individuals who look at her as "special" or gifted she doesn't like to be around. Or those who want to continually ask her questions.

We are now used to having others that have passed over, from the other side of the veil, "hanging" around. There are some special friends she has made on that side who hang around a lot. Others come when thought of. Some come because they know she can see them. Most of the time they are only known to her when they are there. At other times, the rest of us have "experienced" them at our home. After three plus years of having her live in both worlds, it has become old hat for our family. There are many occasions when we do have fun with it and interact with those who are passed on, through her. I guess to some people that may seem a bit odd or weird, yet to us now it is quite normal.

Organizations to Contact

American Association of Retired Persons (AARP)
601 E St. NW, Washington, DC   20049
(888) 687-2277
Web site: www.aarp.org

AARP is a nonprofit, nonpartisan membership organization for people aged fifty and older that is dedicated to enhancing quality of life for all people as they age. AARP provides a grief and loss section on its Web site that offers publications about being alone, dealing with final details, and the loss of various family members.

American Association of Suicidology (AAS)
5221 Wisconsin Ave. NW, Washington, DC   20015
(202) 237-2280 • fax: (202) 237-2282
e-mail: info@suicidology.org
Web site: www.suicidology.org

The goal of AAS is to understand and prevent suicide. AAS sponsors several conferences each year to educate the public about suicide prevention and healing for survivors after the suicide of a loved one. The group also publishes the bimonthly journal *Suicide and Life-Threatening Behavior*, two quarterly newsletters, and a directory of suicide prevention and crisis intervention agencies in the United States.

The American Foundation for Suicide Prevention (AFSP)
120 Wall St., 22nd Floor., New York, NY   10005
(888) 333-AFSP • fax: (212) 363-6237
e-mail: inquiry@afsp.org
Web site: www.afsp.org

AFSP is the only national not-for-profit organization exclusively dedicated to funding research, developing prevention initiatives, and offering educational programs and conferences for suicide survivors, mental health professionals, physicians, and the public. The foundation's activities include supporting research projects that help further the understanding and treatment of depression and the prevention of suicide, providing information and education about depression and suicide, and promoting professional education for the recognition and treatment of depressed and suicidal individuals. AFSP offers educational brochures, a quarterly newsletter, and a frequently-asked-questions section on its Web site.

The Association for Death Education and Counseling (ADEC)
60 Revere Dr., Ste. 500, Northbrook, IL   60062
(847) 509-0403 • fax: (847) 480-9282
e-mail: info@adec.org
Web site: www.adec.org

The ADEC is an international professional organization dedicated to promoting excellence in death education, care of the dying, and bereavement counseling and support. The association provides information, support, and resources to its members and the public. ADEC offers numerous educational opportunities through its annual conference, courses, and workshops, its certification program, and the newsletter *Forum*. ADEC also publishes five journals, *Omega: Journal of Death and Dying*, *Death Studies*, *Journal of Trauma and Loss*, *Living with Loss*, and *Mortality Journal*.

Bereaved Parents of the USA (BP/USA)
National Office, Park Forest, IL   60466
(708) 748-7866
Web site: www.bereavedparentsusa.org

Bereaved Parents of the USA is a national nonprofit self-help group that offers support to bereaved parents, grandparents, and siblings struggling to recover from the death of their loved ones to suicide. It has chapters around the country that hold monthly meetings, publish monthly newsletters, and maintain lending libraries for their members' use. BP/USA conducts yearly national gatherings where bereaved families attend workshops, sharing sessions, and lectures by guest speakers on many aspects of grief. BP/USA publishes a quarterly national newsletter and has several helpful brochures available (in English and Spanish) on its Web site.

Bereavement Services
Gunderson Lutheran Medical Foundation, La Crosse, WI
  54601
(608) 775-4747 • fax: (608) 775-5137
e-mail: info@bereavementservices.org
Web site: www.bereavementservices.org

Bereavement Services is the leading national and international provider of bereavement training and support services for professionals who care for bereaved families, especially regarding the loss of a pregnancy or child. Bereavement Services provides access to a newsletter about perinatal loss and offers a catalog of brochures and booklets pertaining to all aspects of grief.

Citizens United Resisting Euthanasia (CURE)
303 Truman St., Berkeley Springs, WV 25411
(304) 258-LIFE/5433
e-mail: cureltd@verizon.net
Web site: www.mysite.verizon.net/cureltd

Founded in 1981, CURE is an international grassroots network of patient advocates from a wide range of professional, political, and religious backgrounds bound together in a common cause: uncompromising opposition to euthanasia. CURE defends the lives of those considered candidates for euthanasia through a broad range of print and online media as well as radio and television broadcasts. CURE provides brochures on various topics related to euthanasia free of charge on its Web site as well as news updates and links to other similar resources.

The Compassionate Friends
PO Box 3696, Oak Brook, IL 60522-3696
(877) 969-0010 • fax: (630) 990-0246

e-mail: nationaloffice@compassionatefriends.org
Web site:www.compassionatefriends.org

The Compassionate Friends is a national nonprofit self-help support organization that offers friendship, understanding, and hope to bereaved parents, grandparents, and siblings. Its mission is to assist families toward the positive resolution of grief following the death of a child of any age. This organization has many resources for the bereaved and publishes brochures and a national magazine focusing on specific kinds of loss, such as the loss of a child, pregnancy, or sibling.

Death with Dignity National Center (DDNC)
520 SW Sixth Ave., Ste. 1030, Portland, OR   97204
(503) 228-4415 • fax: (503) 228-7454
Web site: www.deathwithdignity.org

The mission of DDNC is to provide information, education, research, and support for the preservation and implementation of the Oregon Death with Dignity law. DDNC activities include efforts to inform and educate the general public and elected government officials about the Oregon Death with Dignity law, to counteract any attempts by opponents to repeal or limit the law, to advocate for improved care and treatment options for the terminally ill, and to promote the Oregon law as a model for other states. Its Web site gives the history and details of the Oregon law that legalizes physician-assisted suicide, an extensive list of direct links to personal stories, relevant books and articles, and a glossary of terms.

Euthanasia Research and Guidance Organization (ERGO)
24829 Norris Ln., Junction City, OR   97448-9559
(541) 998-1873
e-mail: ergo@efn.org
Web site: www.finalexit.org

ERGO is a nonprofit educational corporation that was founded in 1993 to improve the quality of background research on assisted dying for persons who are terminally or hopelessly ill and wish to end their suffering. ERGO develops and publishes ethical, psychological, and legal guidelines for patients and physicians to better prepare them to make life-ending decisions. It also supplies literature to other right-to-die groups worldwide and briefs journalists, authors, and graduate students on the issue. ERGO has a catalog of books, pamphlets, essays, and news stories about euthanasia available on its Web site.

The Hastings Center
21 Malcolm Gordon Rd., Garrison, NY   10524-5555
(845) 424-4040 • fax: (845) 424-4545
e-mail: mail@thehastingscenter.org
Web site: www.hastingscenter.org

The Hastings Center is an independent, nonpartisan, nonprofit bioethics research institute founded in 1969 to explore fundamental and emerging questions in health care, biotechnology, and the environment. The center conducts research and provides consultations on ethical issues such as assisted suicide and offers a forum for exploration and debate. The center publishes and makes available online books, papers, guidelines, and two bimonthly journals, including the *Hastings Center Report.*

Human Life International (HLI)
4 Family Life Ln., Front Royal, VA   22630
(800) 549-LIFE • fax: (540) 622-6247
e-mail: hli@hli.org
Web site: www.hli.org

The mission of HLI is to promote and defend the sanctity of life and family around the world according to the teachings of the Roman Catholic Church through prayer, service, and education. It offers positive alternatives to abortion, assisted suicide, and euthanasia. In fulfilling this mission HLI strives to train, organize, and equip pro-life leaders worldwide. The group publishes the monthly journal *Special Report* and a quarterly magazine and offers access to commentaries and press releases online.

International Association for Near Death Studies (IANDS)
PO Box 502, East Windsor Hill, CT   06028-0502
(860) 882-1211 • fax: (860) 882-1212
Web site: www.iands.org

IANDS promotes exploration of near-death and near-death-like experiences, their effects on people's lives, and their implications for beliefs about life, death, and human purpose. IANDS sponsors support groups, funds research, provides continuing education programs, and maintains a speaker's bureau. It publishes two quarterly periodicals, the scholarly *Journal of Near-Death Studies, Vital Signs* in addition to other informational and research materials.

International Task Force on Euthanasia and Assisted Suicide (ITF)
PO Box 760, Steubenville, OH   43952
(740) 282-3810
Web site: www.iaetf.org

The goal of ITF is to make certain that a patient's right to receive care and compassion is not replaced by a doctor's right to prescribe poison or administer a lethal injection. It offers fact sheets, answers to frequently asked questions about euthanasia and assisted suicide, and books such as *Power over Pain: How to Get the Pain Control You Need, Culture of Death: The Assault on Medical Ethics in America, Deadly Compassion: The Death of Ann Humphrey and the Truth About Euthanasia,* and *Forced Exit: The Slippery Slope from Assisted Suicide to Legalized Murder.*

National Hospice and Palliative Care Organizations (NHPCO)
1700 Diagonal Rd., Ste. 625, Alexandria, VA   22314
(703) 837-1500 • fax: (703) 837-1233
caringinfo@nhpco.org
Web site: www.nhpco.org

The NHPCO is the largest nonprofit membership organization representing hospice and palliative care programs and professionals in the United States. The organization is committed to improving end-of-life care and expanding access to hospice care with the goal of profoundly enhancing quality of life for dying people and their loved ones in America. Its Web site provides materials about end-of-life care, including brochures on grief, advance directives, end-of-life caregiving, dying at home, and information for caregivers providing care for dying patients.

Near Death Experience Research Foundation (NDERF)
PO Box 23367, Federal Way, WA   98093
fax: (253) 568-7778
e-mail: nderf@nderf.org
Web site: www.nderf.org

NDERF provides information, education, and research regarding near-death experiences. Its Web site contains more than three hundred personal stories of near-death experiences in multiple languages, an extensive list of books and reviews on this topic, and multimedia presentations of near-death experiences. The Web site also includes current journal articles, bulletin boards, and chat rooms for people to post descriptions of their near-death experiences.

Share Pregnancy and Infant Loss Support
National Share Office, St. Charles, MO   63301-2893
(800) 821-6819 • fax: (636) 947-7486
e-mail: share@nationalshareoffice.com
Web site: www.nationalshareoffice.com

The mission of Share Pregnancy and Infant Loss Support is to serve those whose lives are touched by the tragic death of a baby through early pregnancy loss, stillbirth, or death in the first few months of life. Share offers a catalog of audio, video, and written materials on subjects such as fathers' grief, siblings' grief, and subsequent pregnancy after the loss of a child. The Web site also offers advice about how to plan a memorial service for a pregnancy or infant loss, access to the group's newsletter, information about upcoming conferences and events, and information about local Share support groups.

Web Sites

Focus Adolescent Services
www.focusas.com

Focus Adolescent Services is a Web site clearinghouse of information and resources on teen and family issues to help and support families with troubled and at-risk teens. The grief and bereavement portion of this Web site includes articles, information about other support organizations, recommended readings on child and adolescent grief, an information and referral telephone line for families of troubled teens, and a list of warning signs that may indicate that a teen is having serious difficulty with grief and loss.

InterLIFE—The Euthanasia Corner
www.interlife.org

InterLIFE is a project of the "Life Web site" Society, a small nonprofit group that seeks to combat the "culture of death" with the "culture of life." The site offers reports, essays, and opinions by those with an antieuthanasia perspective and posts news updates and court decisions on euthanasia cases.

For Further Research

Books

Lewis R. Aiken, *Dying, Death, and Bereavement*. Mahwah, NJ: Lawrence Erlbaum, 2001.

Michael Berman, *Parenthood Lost: Healing the Pain After Miscarriage, Stillbirth, and Infant Death*. Westport, CT: Bergin & Garvey, 2001.

Clifton D. Bryant, *Handbook of Death and Dying*. Thousand Oaks, CA: Sage, 2003.

Moira Cairns, *Transitions in Dying and Bereavement: A Psychosocial Guide for Hospice and Palliative Care*. Baltimore: Health Professions, 2003.

Bonnie Effros, *Caring for Body and Soul*. University Park: Pennsylvania State University Press, 2002.

Mark Fox, *Religion, Spirituality and the Near-Death Experience*. London: Routledge, 2003.

Bert Hayslip Jr. and Cynthia A. Peveto, *Cultural Changes in Attitudes Toward Death, Dying and Bereavement*. New York: Springer, 2005.

Jenny Hockey, Jeanne Katz, and Neil Small, *Grief, Mourning and Death Ritual*. Philadelphia: Open University Press, 2001.

Glennys Howarth and Oliver Leaman, *Encyclopedia of Death and Dying*. London: Routledge, 2001.

Elisabeth Kübler-Ross, *Living with Death and Dying*. New York: Macmillan, 1981.

Shai J. Lavi, *The Modern Art of Dying: A History of Euthanasia in the United States*. Princeton, NJ: Princeton University Press, 2005.

Claudio Lomnitz, *Death and the Idea of Mexico*. Brooklyn, NY: Zone, 2005.

Susan Orpett Long, *Final Days: Japanese Culture and Choice at the End of Life*. Honolulu: University of Hawaii Press, 2005.

Raymond Moody Jr., *Life After Life: The Investigation of a Phenomenon—Survival of Bodily Death*. Harrisburg, PA: Stackpole, 1976.

Joan K. Parry and Angela Shell Ryan, *A Cross-Cultural Look at Death, Dying, and Religion*. Chicago: Nelson-Hall, 1995.

Richard P. Taylor, *Death and the Afterlife: A Cultural Encyclopedia*. Santa Barbara, CA: ABC-CLIO, 2000.

Periodicals

Miriam J. Anderson, Samuel J. Marwit, Brian Vandenburg, and John T. Chibnall, "Psychological and Religious Coping Strategies of Mothers Bereaved by the Sudden Death of a Child," *Death Studies*, November 2005.

Rachel Bletchly, "Little Kirsty Doesn't Know She's Dying," *People Weekly*, April 23, 2000.

Deborah Carr, "A 'Good Death' for Whom? Quality of Spouse's Death and Psychological Distress Among Older Widowed Persons," *Journal of Health and Social Behavior*, June 2003.

Victor G. Cicirelli, "Fear of Death in Mid–Old Age," *Journals of Gerontology: Psychological Sciences and Social Sciences*, March 2006.

Laura Crow, "Extreme Measures: A Personal Story of Letting Go," *Death Studies*, March 2006.

Lesley C. Dinwiddie, "Be Not Afraid: Overcoming the Fear of Death," *Nephrology Nursing Journal*, April 2003.

Yulia Chentsova Dutton and Sidney Zisook, "Adaptation to Bereavement," *Death Studies*, December 2005.

Healthcare Mergers, Acquisitions and Ventures Week, "National Taiwan University Hospital; Fear of Death Among Young and Elderly with Terminal Cancers in Taiwan Examined," July 9, 2005.

Richard T. Hull, "The Case For: Physician-Assisted Suicide," *Free Inquiry*, Spring 2003.

Gerald E. Kreyche, "Death—the Final Frontier," *USA Today* magazine, May 2002.

Amy Hui-Mei Huang Lin, "Factors Related to Attitudes Toward Death Among Americans and Chinese Older Adults," *Omega*, vol. 47, no. 1, 2003.

Mirror, "Sry I Kild Myself: Suicide Victims Text Final Words to Loved Ones," February 13, 2006.

Richard J. Mularski et al., "Agreement Among Family Members in Their Assessment of the Quality of Dying and Death," *Journal of Pain and Symptom Management*, October 2004.

Robert A. Neimeyer, Joachim Wittkowski, and Richard Moser, "Psychological Research on Death Attitudes: An Overview and Evaluation," *Death Studies*, May 2004.

Donald L. Patrick et al., "Measuring and Improving the Quality of Dying and Death," *Annals of Internal Medicine*, September 2003.

Ingmar Persson, "Human Death: A View from the Beginning of Life," *Bioethics*, February 2002.

Jean-Robert Pitte, "A Short Cultural Geography of Death and the Dead," *GeoJournal*, December 2004.

Gary Ralston, "Body of Evidence: Scientists May Soon Have Proof of Life After Death," *Glasgow Daily Record*, February 23, 2001.

Wesley J. Smith, "Angels of Death: Exploring the Euthanasia Underground," *First Things: A Monthly Journal of Religion and Public Life*, November 2002.

Society for the Advancement of Education, "Women Less Likely Than Men to Commit Suicide," *USA Today* magazine, April 2001.

Studs Terkel, "Will the Circle Be Unbroken? Interviews with a Paramedic, a Social Worker, an Undertaker and a Mother About Their Experiences with Death and Dying," *Atlantic Monthly* October 2001.

Stefan Timmermans, "Death Brokering: Constructing Culturally Appropriate Deaths," *Sociology of Health and Illness*, November 2005.

James VanOosting, "Death and Resurrection," *Humanist*, November/December 2002.

Paul Wink and Julia Scott, "Does Religiousness Buffer Against the Fear of Death and Dying in Late Adulthood? Findings from a Longitudinal Study," *Journals of Gerontology: Psychological Sciences and Social Sciences*, July 2005.

Kristin Wright, "Relationships with Death: The Terminally Ill Talk About Dying," *Journal of Marital and Family Therapy*, October 2003.

Eunja Yeun, "Attitudes of Elderly Korean Patients Towards Death and Dying: An Application of Q-Methodology," *International Journal of Nursing Studies*, November 2005.

Alice G. Yick, "Chinese Cultural Dimensions of Death, Dying and Bereavement: Focus Group Findings," *Journal of Cultural Diversity*, Summer 2002.

Index